JESUS

THE PEOPLE'S CHOICE

Greg Asimakoupoulos
Foreword by Lon Allison

MAINSTAY CHURCH RESOURCES
Wheaton, Illinois

Jesus: The People's Choice

Cover design by De Leon Design
Interior design and composition by Design Corps
Cover photo courtesy of Christ Community Church, St. Charles,
Illinois.

Printed in the United States of America.

ISBN: 1-57849-172-X

Sections of Chapter Two reprinted from the pamphlet "Prejudice:
What's in a Name?" by Greg Asimakoupoulos, copyright © 1999 by
Mainstay Church Resources.

Unless otherwise indicated, all Scripture quotations are taken from the
Holy Bible, New International Version (NIV). Copyright © 1973, 1978,
1984 by the International Bible Society. Used by permission of
Zondervan Publishing House. All rights reserved.

Scriptures noted *The Message* are taken from THE MESSAGE, copyright
© 1993, 1994, 1995, 1996. Used by permission of NavPress Publishing
Group.

Scriptures noted KJV are taken from the King James Version.

Visit our web site at www.helpingpastors.com.

The People's Choice

Two thumbs up!
The hands-down favorite!
Jesus was The People's Choice!
He gave a voice to those involuntarily silenced
by power, prejudice, and unjust dealings.
Stealing the show from the religious professionals,
he staged a performance
of integrity, tough love, and mercy
like the world has never seen since.

But it wasn't a performance.
It was the real thing!
Though rejected by some,
he remained connected and directed
by the One who elected him Messiah.

And because of the unexpected ending
to his weekend waltz with death,
his dance of life continues
with his status undenied.

—Greg E. Asimakoupoulos

CONTENTS

Foreword

THE BOOK TITLE INTRIGUES ME. So does the author.
I've known him for more than 20 years and am
amazed at the gifts of pastor and poet he possess-
es. Therefore, it's a pleasure to write the foreword
for Greg Asimakoupoulos's book, *Jesus: The
People's Choice.*

Not often does a Christian resource book
keep me up late at night and call to me early in
the morning. But this book did. Further, as a
resource to the 50-Day Spiritual Adventure, *Jesus:
The People's Choice* offers insights that will, when
read devotionally and used in a small group setting, drive Christ-principles deep into our character. Quite honestly, I can't wait to use the book in
our church and talk through the ideas in it with
my 50-Day Adventure men's small group.

The people at Mainstay Church Resources,
including this book's author, decided to gamble a
bit with this concept. I first heard about it over
lunch at Baker's Square with David and Karen
Mains and Greg Asimakoupoulos. They wanted
to try using modern-day parables to illumine the
life of Jesus. They didn't write these parables;
they unearthed them in the modern media.
Thus, as you study the life of Christ in each
chapter, scenes from films or shows most of us
have seen or at least heard about become the
"A farmer went out to sow" stories, illustrating
Christ's life and principles.

I liked the idea. Like them, I observe that the
media is the dominant roadway of cultural

expression for most people in our country. Wherever I speak evangelistically, I go in knowing that I can draw from modern movies and videos to show humankind's needs and aspirations. From there, I move as quickly as possible to Jesus, who is the complete answer to both the perceived and hidden cries of the human heart. So in each chapter of this book, you'll find media parables. The author weaves the parables seamlessly into his concepts.

I had a concern, however, about the "film parable" idea before I read the book. I wondered how well Jesus would stand up against the "star power" of Hollywood's best actors and directors. I didn't know if Greg, despite his considerable writing skills, could elevate Jesus and his life from 2000-year-old dusty pages to stand alongside and in fact dominate the images from Spielberg and Howard. But have no fear. When Jesus is lifted up and the Scriptures are accurately and creatively expounded, he dominates every scene. That is the case with this book. He increased and Hollywood decreased.

Jesus is the light of the world. He is the Morning Star. The author of this book refers to him with light and star metaphors, just like the Scriptures do. But then Greg takes the "light" concept and reminds us that we are lights for our world. Luther called Christians "little Christs." We are Jesus' "little lights" in an increasingly dark world. The book then introduces readers to a strategy that is swiftly captivating the evangelical church in America. The "Lighthouse" strategy calls for believers to make their homes and workplaces lighthouses of the good news of Jesus.

We do this by intentionally praying for the 10 to 20 households near us throughout the year

2000. And, as we pray, we look for ways to care for them and share Christ with them. We can be Christ's shining stars in lighthouses and light-offices and lightfactories throughout the land in the year 2000! It's exciting to think about. We know that if three million Christians form light-houses and pray for twenty households, we have the potential of reaching every person in the U.S.A. through Prayer, Care, and Share ministry.

Starting tonight, August 5, 1999, you'll find a little electric candle burning in the front room window of my home in Palatine, Illinois. It will burn brightly through the year 2000. When our neighbors ask us why, we'll say something like, "The light reminds us that Jesus is this world's light, and we're praying for everyone in our neighborhood to know his light and peace. How can we pray for you?"

I'm convinced this book will encourage you to be just as outspoken about the saving light of Jesus, The People's Choice.

Lon Allison
Director
Billy Graham Center, Wheaton College

Introduction

"MAY I HAVE THE ENVELOPE, PLEASE?"

The dark auditorium grows strangely silent. Excitement hangs heavy in the air. The presenter at the Plexiglas podium reaches for the sealed envelope and tears it open. He clears his throat and reads: *"The winner of the People's Choice Award is . . . Jesus!"*

The spotlight searches the audience to locate a man with an olive complexion. The focused beam follows a bearded rabbi as he ascends the steps to the stage and accepts his award. The crowd stands, whistling and applauding, cheering with unconfined emotion. Jesus smiles. He waves. He closes his eyes and drinks in the adulation as the audience begins to sing,

Thou art worthy,
thou art worthy,
thou art worthy, O Lord.
Thou art worthy to receive glory,
glory and honor and power.

Unthinkable? Don't be too quick to cast a negative ballot. What I've just described is not far from the description we have of heaven in Revelation 4—5. The day will come when the throngs of heaven will break into songs of endless worship as the Lamb of God takes center stage and breaks the seal of the scroll. As he does, he will validate the reason why he is and forever will be "The People's Choice." I can hardly wait.

Now, it is true that since the People's Choice Awards were established in 1974 to give Americans the chance to honor their favorite performers, Jesus has not been one of the winners. For one reason, none of the categories for which 202 million people vote each year include Most Attractive Person. Sure, people cast their vote for their favorite performers. But the person in life who is most *attractive*—who draws people near, sometimes without their even being conscious of the reasons—that person has not been named.

It's just as well. Given the superficial reasons we attach celebrity status to rap artists, talk show hosts, professional athletes, or politicians, the People's Choice crystal award (handcrafted in Sweden and valued at $3000) would be an insult to One who claims a cross as his trophy. For one thing, Jesus is not a performer. He didn't *play* the part of God. He *is* God.

The People's Choice Throughout History

Don't get me wrong. Jesus is a lot more popular than you might think. His importance may be overlooked by some, but not by the majority. During 1999, *Time* magazine conducted an online survey to identify the Person of the Century. The last tabulation I saw showed Jesus Christ in first place, with more than 800,000 votes—despite the fact that he was ineligible for the award by *Time* standards!

One problem we have in celebrating Jesus is getting beyond the way he has been portrayed. Unlike some, who regularly question the reliability of Jesus' words in the Bible, we revere the Scriptures as authoritative. But many of us have failed to see the color in Jesus' eyes, the warmth of his winsome personality, and the brightness of his ready smile. We miss seeing him as a real person—someone we might bump into walking down the street and say, as we come away, "Wow. What a great guy! I really like him!"

I grew up in the church. My dad was a pastor. My mom taught Sunday school, played the organ, and led the youth group. We were at church constantly. So, from the time I was in diapers, I was exposed to pictures of Jesus. In our home, Bible storybooks and Sunday school papers were as common as Mother Goose collections.

Almost without exception, the pictures of Jesus in those books left me feeling uneasy. Vacant. Somber. Fragile. Hardly an image fitting the daring exploits I heard each week at church. You know—the Jesus who spent six weeks alone in the desert surrounded by wild animals, who rearranged furniture in the temple in a fit of anger, who was equally at home near a carpenter's bench and in the back of a boat bouncing around in a storm. The Jesus who didn't run for cover after calling the religious bigshots of Jerusalem a bunch of whitewashed tombstones.

Like layers of varnish on a treasured antique tend to hide the beauty of the natural wood grain, traditional treatments of the life of Christ often hide the simplicity that accounts for his winsome magnetism and enduring popularity. The 50-Day Spiritual Adventure, for which this little book is written, will help you uncover some transferable principles that have been overlooked for too long.

Ever hear of praying with a pencil? Once, while sitting in silence in an attitude of prayer, I pulled out a pad of paper and a pencil and began to paint a word portrait of Jesus that had eluded me as a child. The result is an image I can't get out of my head:

> A bearded man of thirty with tanned skin sits on a green grassy hillside overlooking a midnight-blue sea. With his callused hands, he holds a toddler on his lap. Other older children crowd near him, singing and giggling while he tousles their hair and laughs. His eyes sparkle. It's obvious he loves children. And, convinced of his unconditional love, it's just as obvious the children adore this man. But not only the children. As my mind's eye pans the wider scene, there are more than children in this picture. Thousands of people come into view, huddled on the hillside within earshot of this young prophet. If you look closely, you see the variety of people represented: the strong and the frail; the young, middle-aged, and elderly; women, men, and children; those scarred by abuse; prominent leaders; the homeless and the marginalized; those religiously inclined and the avowed atheists.

People of all ages and backgrounds loved Jesus. They flocked to him. As you read the four New Testament Gospels that record the life of Christ, you see that Jesus often told people not to say anything about him. His fear was that word would spread and crowds would gather, hindering his ability to circulate around the country and reach as many people as possible. On more than one occasion, Jesus was forced to leave a location in the middle of the night in order to escape the masses. An eyewitness of his Palm

Sunday entrance into Jerusalem records the reaction of our Lord's critics, who were astounded at his popularity. "The whole world has gone after him!" they said (John 12:19). Without question, there was something about this Someone that attracted people.

Jesus used creative principles to effectively connect with people. For instance, he illustrated the ideas he communicated using contemporary images and simple stories people could understand with little effort—the parables. In our culture—where Academy and People's Choice Awards are pulses of our values—television, videos, and movies are those images. I strongly believe the language of Hollywood is the common language of our culture. If we are going to connect with those who know about Jesus but have not yet found reason to celebrate his Lordship, we must learn to speak their language. Consequently, throughout this book, I have used several references to plays, films, or videos you may have seen or heard of.

Theatergoing is not mandatory to fully appreciate the impact of this book or to take part in the "Screen Your Message" action step. I know not all Christians feel at home in the theater. Some have opted not to see movies as a way of protesting the questionable content of certain Hollywood offerings. For many folks, it is simply a matter of conscience. Others wait until specific films are available on video so they can be viewed at home privately, where offensive scenes can be skipped. And many, many sincere Christians find that a good film not only provides a means of relaxation but also is a source of theological reflection that enriches their spiritual life and, more importantly to my purposes in this book, offers a bridge to those who have yet to cross over into kingdom territory.

That's the way Jesus used the "media" of his day. A runaway son, a greedy farmer, and a careless traveler attacked by thieves made perfect characters for his stories. While the more religious people back then couldn't relate to references of squandering, avarice, and violence, the common people—those he was really trying to reach—*could* relate. And they found him incredibly appealing.

The People's Choice Today

He was The People's Choice then and he continues to be. Do you know how many times Jesus has been featured on *Time* magazine's cover in recent years? I've lost count, but I have four of those covers displayed in my office. The public is fascinated with him as much now as they ever were. Every time a survey is taken of most-admired people, Jesus makes the list. And the admiration of him by his followers, who call themselves *Christians*, only continues to grow.

Call it a Jesus movement. Call it a spiritual awakening. Bill Bright, founder of Campus Crusade for Christ, calls it a revival. Evelyn Christensen of United Prayer Ministry calls it a gathering army. Whatever you call it, don't overlook the attention Jesus is getting as we enter a new millennium.

Students in unprecedented numbers are assembling at public school flagpoles to pray for their teachers and fellow students and to take a stand for Jesus. In the tragic 1999 high-school shooting in Littleton, Colorado, seventeen-year-old Cassie Bernall took just such a stand. "Do you believe in God?" one of the teenage gunmen asked her when he found her reading the Bible in Columbine High School's library. Cassie bravely replied, "Yes, I believe in God," and was shot and killed. And in 1997, 1.5 million men and boys converged as Promise Keepers in Washington, D.C., to "stand in the gap" for the values articulated by the Son of God.

According to Mission America, a coalition of 74 denominations and 300 parachurch ministries, churches large and small aren't as turf-conscious as they've been in the past. Instead, in major cities across North America, congregations of every imaginable denomination are viewing themselves as individual classrooms composing one church. Pastors see themselves as Sunday school teachers in a unified citywide church measured by square miles, not by the length and breadth of an individual sanctuary.

As your church, along with hundreds of thousands of other churches, celebrates Jesus over the coming year, you will be invited to think creatively about what it means to share your faith with people who are spiritually apathetic in your family, neighborhood, and workplace. In the following chapters, you will be reminded of the unique approaches Jesus used to call attention to God's kingdom. My hope is that you will be inspired to rethink your own approach in light of what proved so effective for our Leader. I also hope to whet your appetite with ways you can celebrate the attractiveness of our Savior, so those in your sphere of influence will have their interest piqued.

If you're ready, turn the page, and let's celebrate Jesus—The People's Choice!

A Cup of Communion

Alone with the Father
at the start of each day,
he quieted his heart
starving all ambition.
Listening.
Praying.
Pondering God's will.
Standing still.
Kneeling down.
Looking up.
Taking a cup,
he swallowed his pride
and drank in his Father's love.

—gea

CHAPTER
ONE

Taking His Cues from the Director

BEFORE THE EASTERN HORIZON loosened its grip on darkness, long before a rooster called a new day to attention, a solitary figure was seen silhouetted against the early morning sky. Those who knew him knew where to find him. Early each morning, as the night prepared to pass the baton on to a new day, he was either kneeling at a large boulder, reclining against the trunk of a ancient olive tree, or walking the beach with his face tilted toward heaven. It wasn't that the man couldn't sleep. The truth is, he knew he couldn't keep in step with his life mission without his daily pre-dawn routine.

Those who observed Jesus made mention of his practice. "Very early in the morning, while it was still dark, Jesus got up, left the house and went off to a solitary place, where he prayed" (Mark 1:35).

Jesus stayed spiritually connected and directed.

When I read that verse, I think of my father. My dad pastored small churches in the Pacific Northwest while I was growing up. One of the

joys of my life as an elementary school kid was
getting to visit Dad in his study at the church.
He'd be perched at his manual typewriter, pounding away on his sermon outline. Commentaries
and books and magazines relating to the theme
of his message covered his desk. Laying on his
lap was his brown, leather-bound *Thompson
Chain Reference* King James Bible. It was opened
to the passage he was meditating on as he typed.
I loved to hear my dad pour out his heart in
audible prayer to the Lord. My presence didn't
hinder him from unloading his concerns, fears,
hurts, and hopes.

Because of a medical condition and financial
constraints on our family, Dad left fulltime pastoring when I entered junior high school. But the
disciplines he had developed during his 20 years
as a pastor continued to guide his life. Every
morning, before anyone in our house was up, my
father would brew a pot of coffee and sit in the
black leather chair in the corner of the family
room to meet with his Father. His well-marked
brown Bible was in one hand, a cup of French
roast coffee in the other. A stack of commentaries
he was studying were within arm's reach. Before
showering or shaving or letting the dog out, my
dad spent large chunks of time with the Lord
each day, even though he didn't have a sermon
to prepare. He still does.

Every August when our family takes a vaca-
tion, I have a chance to travel from Illinois to
Washington to visit my aging parents. I bounce
out of bed early to get some exercise, but not
nearly early enough to be the first one up. The
coffee is made, and there in the corner chair my
dad is getting his daily direction from the
Director of his soul. That image of my father in

his bathrobe seated in his chair with his open Bible is tattooed on my brain. I will treasure that memory long after he's gone.

My dad's example has enabled me to share, to a certain degree, the disciples' experience as they watched Jesus maintain his commitment to be spiritually connected to his Father. This was his means to be clearly directed in what he did, what he said, where he went, and with whom he spent time.

A Nourishing Connection

The scene in Mark 1 throbs with excitement. Jesus demonstrated his power over disease and demons. The word began to travel along the beach cities of Galilee. The crowds rushed in on him nonstop. There was no time to eat. The days were long; the nights were longer. Eventually Peter's mother-in-law, herself the recipient of a miracle, convinced Jesus and the others that they needed some nourishment. As they went off to bed, the disciples began to make plans for a major evangelistic crusade right there in Capernaum. They were experiencing the same kind of rush that campaign organizers feel when their candidate is winning by a landslide. And in the morning, at the crack of dawn, they were ready to go rent the largest hall in town.

But where was Jesus? He was not in the house. He was not at the beach. The crowds they'd turned away the night before were already lined up at the door to Peter's home. But Jesus was missing. Finally, the disciples found him on a solitary hillside. To their amazement, Jesus was not interested in their plans for an extended revival. In his quiet contemplation with the Father, the Son had clarified his game plan for the day.

Even though it seems nonsensical to turn your back on a receptive audience, that is exactly what Jesus knew he had to do. As much as he may have enjoyed the tantalizing flavor of hot unleavened bread fresh out of the oven, as much as he might have developed a fancy for the sweetness of success, Jesus longed even more for the satisfying taste of doing the will of God. That was his nourishment. And he knew in order to do what the Father demanded, he continually had to connect with him.

> **In his quiet contemplation with the Father, the Son had clarified his game plan for the day.**

What comes just prior to this scene in the Gospel of Mark is Jesus' lonely trek in the Judean wilderness. Following his baptism by his cousin John in the Jordan River, Jesus voluntarily denied himself contact with people or food. It was a fast that would eventually take its toll, if a person were only accustomed to partaking of physical nourishment. But Jesus had another source of sustenance. For 40 days he connected with his Father. They communed together, as was their custom in the realm of eternity before the Son took on human skin and entered our sinful planet. During those uninterrupted moments of spiritual refreshment, Jesus walked the rugged terrain of a windswept desert. As he listened to his Father's voice, Jesus charted out the steps he would follow in his public ministry.

Oh yes, there were those three interruptions near the end of his solitary retreat. Satan slithered amid the craggy cliffs, tempting Jesus. It shouldn't surprise us that one way the enemy attempted to entice him was by playing on his obvious hunger. Pointing to flat stones that no doubt resembled unleavened bread (if you've ever been to Israel, you know there are stones like that everywhere), Satan challenged Jesus to transform them to bread. His approach was similar with the two other temptations. But Jesus didn't budge.

For years I viewed this passage with the belief that Jesus could barely resist the tempter's offer. Recently my coworker Dan Lupton helped me see my interpretation of the temptation episode might not be right. "Since he'd been fasting for nearly six weeks, certainly Jesus was starved for food and human companionship," Dan smiled. "But, don't think for a minute he was on the verge of giving in. After all, he was on a spiritual high. Anyone who has prayed and fasted for an extended season discovers unprecedented moral strength through an indescribable intimacy with God."

No wonder Jesus chose to maintain his daily regimen after breaking his fast and entering the public eye. To sever Jesus from the life source within him would have undermined the power and strength that made him unique. His ability to act in accordance with God's mission for his life hinged on daily contact with heaven. He had tasted firsthand what was required to resist invitations to compromise his integrity.

We see a reflection of that principle in the story of Eric Liddell. Nicknamed "The Flying Scotsman," Eric was one of Great Britain's fastest athletes. In the 1924 Olympics, he won the gold medal for the 400-meter race. *Chariots of Fire,* the film that garnered Best Picture glories at the 1981 Academy Awards, tells his God-honoring story.

Raised by Presbyterian missionaries in China, Eric felt called to the same vocation. But he also loved to run. One reason he loved it so much was his speed. In a poignant dialogue in the movie, Eric's sister Jenny somberly chides her brother for allowing athletics to interfere with his call to the mission field. He counters, "Oh, Jen, don't you see? God made me fast. And when I run, I feel his pleasure!" For Eric, competing in track-and-field events was part of his call. The Divine Director sat in his captain's chair, shouting through a megaphone, "On your mark, get set, go!" And as Eric flew, his heavenly Father beamed with pride.

> **The Divine Director sat in his captain's chair, shouting through a megaphone, "On your mark, get set, go!"**

But Eric had personal convictions that grew out of his relationship with Jesus Christ. He refused to compete on Sundays. For the Liddell family, and for Eric in particular, a solemn observance of the Sabbath was not a legalistic prescription as much as it was a privilege. It sustained their sense of spiritual connection and direction.

If you saw *Chariots of Fire,* you know the predicament Eric's personal code put him in. As a twenty-two-year-old student at the University of Edinburgh, he had been chosen to represent Great Britain in the Paris Olympic games. The 100 meters was his race; he had validated his ownership of the 100 meters time and time again. But when the schedule of events was posted, Eric was dismayed to learn the 100 meters would be run on a Sunday. Although disappointed, he did not hesitate to announce his inability to compete.

In the film version of the story, the Olympic committee of Great Britain then arranges to meet with Eric at a posh Paris hotel. Their desire is to find a way to get the "religious fanatic" to reverse his decision. They bait the hook with enticing options. Eric, in a crowded room, feels alone. But Jesus Christ, who dwells within him, had been in such a wilderness-like setting before. Having exercised his spiritual muscles through prayer and meditation as much as he has exercised his body, Eric doesn't panic. He knows what to do. Liddell stands by his beliefs. The committee burns with rage. Their hopes of Scottish gold in the 100 meters vanish before their eyes, along with the circling smoke of their Cuban cigars. At just that moment, Lord Andrew Lindsay, a member of the British team, enters the room and proposes a solution to the dilemma. Since he has already medalled in the hurdles, he is willing to give up his spot in the 400 meters to be run on Thursday. Eric smiles. The committee breathes a sigh of relief.

Then there is a most telling conversation between two of the committee members reflecting on Eric's firm decision not to run on Sunday and their attempt to change his mind. They conclude it would have been terribly wrong if they had succeeded in tempting Eric. "The lad, as you call him, is a true man of principle and a true athlete. His speed is a mere extension of his life and its force. We sought to sever his running from his self."

If Eric Liddell had given in to the pressure to run on Sunday, it's likely he would not have won. Likewise, if Jesus had given in to the pressure to stay in Capernaum and respond to those who had been unable to see him the night

before, his effectiveness would have been compromised. He knew in his heart what he needed
to do. It was time to move on. Jesus had learned
how to hear the voice of his Father.

Spiritual Junk Food

One of the reasons we have difficulty staying
spiritually directed is because we struggle to stay
spiritually connected. In nearly 20 years of pastoring, I have gained insight into the reason for
this. It seems many committed Christians, who
would be quick to wear a campaign button saying Jesus is their choice, don't spend time with
him discussing problems or reading what he
believes on the issues. Instead, they rely on what
others tell them.

Do you know why the notorious bears of
Yellowstone Park aren't as visible as they used to
be? Well, over the years, these furry creatures
were not only being photographed by wide-eyed
tourists, they were also being fed by them. And
the food offered was quite different from their
natural diet of nuts, berries, fish, and small animals. The resulting consequences were tragic.

During hibernation, the fat buildup from
"people food" burned off much more rapidly
than the normal animal fat created by a bear's
natural diet. Throughout the winter months,
scores of bruins froze to death. So the bears were
relocated by truck to the high country, away
from tourist trails.

I wonder how many Christians are in need of
being relocated to the high country, where their
daily diet of discipleship can be assured? Just as
bears must be guarded against the wrong kind of
food, we must guard against the wrong kind of
spiritual nourishment. For lack of a better term,

I'm calling this *spiritual junk food.* By this term, I mean a secondhand reliance on faith, living our Christianity through other people. We hope certain folks we respect and admire will continue to live close to God and experience his power. Then all we have to do is simply draw close to them. It works, right? Well, if that's all we ever do, we never get to know God ourselves.

> **Just as bears must be guarded against the wrong kind of food, we must guard against the wrong kind of spiritual nourishment.**

Spiritual junk food is whatever curbs our appetite for God himself—those things that fill us up without providing the nutritional value our soul requires in order to remain healthy. It might mean just going to church on Sunday morning and punching the "one-hour-a-week time clock." You get your fill, but if that's all you get, those calories can be pretty empty. Watching Christian TV can be very inspirational, but if all you do is watch other people talk about their walk with the Lord, you are in danger of malnutrition.

A spiritual-junk-food "high" can also result from eating an unbalanced diet of healthy foods. We all benefit from devotional booklets and the Christian books that line our bookcases or nightstands. I have a friend who reads the popular pamphlet *Our Daily Bread.* But if she never read the Bread of Life found between the covers of her Bible, she'd lack a balanced diet only God's Word can provide. Many also have been tremendously helped by television preachers and religious teachers on the radio. But, while these authors and gifted communicators help us understand the Bible and its practical truths, if their insights are all we rely on, we never develop the ability to digest for ourselves what comes from chewing on God's Word and drinking in his presence in prayer.

Spiritual junk food is tasty and easy to come by. But you know as well as I do that if you eat a lot of fast food, it begins to taste like the cardboard cartons it comes in. The same thing is true with Christian media and literature that is high in sugar and fat but lacks the natural fiber of firsthand exposure to the living God. No matter how satisfying spiritual junk food may seem, that which is not obtained through personal discovery is sure to burn off quickly and lose its value in the face of personal testing. Nothing can take the place of firsthand study of the Bible and personal communication with God in prayer. No one can live our faith for us. Christianity cannot be lived vicariously through a pastor, a best friend, or anyone else.

God created us to be nourished personally through his Word, just as he intended the bears in Yellowstone National Park to eat from his creation. As the bear who has eaten well survives the winter, the Christian who is nourished by God's words in Scripture and his whispers in prayer withstands the "winters" of life.

Nurturing a growing relationship doesn't just happen. It requires taking the initiative. Nurturing your relationship with your mate or your best friend involves an investment of time, energy, and sensitivity. The same goes for your relationship with the Lord. It requires talking to him, listening to him, and spending time with him.

How good are you at sensing God's direction for your day? your week? your life? Do you let life just show up at your door each morning and then respond to its random demands? Or do you have purposeful confidence in what you should be about? Can you tell the difference between the urgent and the important? You don't need to be the Son of God to train your heart to be proactively aware of God's direction. It can be as easy as keeping current in your Adventure Journal as you protect the pattern of personal Bible study, reflection, and prayer during this season of accelerated spiritual growth.

> You don't need to be the Son of God to train your heart to be proactively aware of God's direction.

The benefits of such discipline were obvious in the life of a young Lutheran pastor who lived in a turbulent period in Germany. Dietrich Bonhoeffer was a unmarried minister who discovered his relational needs could be met in a structured setting of Christians living in community. He shared his discoveries in a little book I keep on my shelf of "re-reads."

In *Life Together*, Bonhoeffer warns us to beware of those who are not meaningfully connected to a company of committed believers. He also cautions us to be wary of those who cannot be alone with themselves. With uncanny wisdom, this young theologian asserts that when we are alone with ourselves and God, we learn lessons we cannot learn in a group, thereby obtaining spiritual insights we can share when we are in the presence of others. By the same token, Bonhoeffer claims, it is in companionship with others that we are nourished with the resources we will need when we have to go it alone.

For Dietrich Bonhoeffer, forced aloneness would soon become a reality. Because he was unwilling to compromise his pulpit and preach a version of the gospel filtered through the values of the Third Reich, he was eventually arrested and imprisoned. But he didn't waste away. He was able to feast on the fruit of a faith he stored on the shelf of memory, harvested in Christian community. He had also learned to nourish his soul through a disciplined practice of solitary worship and reflection, so he did not crumble in the crucible of a Nazi concentration camp. From his lonely cell, he shared his learning from intimate times with the Lord with Christians around the world.

Pray with a Pencil

Dietrich Bonhoeffer's example encouraged me when I began my theological studies. I appreciated the fact that his single status had not disqualified him from pastoring. (I was a bachelor for the first four years of my ministry.) His book *Life Together* taught me that the means to survive spiritually in the face of difficulties are incubated in protected times of honest intimacy with the Father.

My first year of seminary was one of the hardest years of my life. The courses I took were both challenging and deeply satisfying. I lived with eight other seminarians in a quaint old home in Pasadena, California, and I was experiencing a level of Christian community I'd only read about. I could personally attest to the blessings of "belonging" about which Bonhoeffer wrote. But as I began to take my calling to ministry seriously, I dealt with issues of spiritual warfare on a level I had not experienced before. I could sense my vulnerability to various kinds of temptation. I battled homesickness and feelings of insecurity. I didn't need a therapist to tell me I was flirting with depression.

Fortunately, one of my professors required us to keep a journal for an entire year. I'd kept a diary since I was eight, so the thought of making daily summaries didn't intimidate me. But what my teacher had in mind was not maintaining a laundry list of what I'd done each day, but a thoughtful chronicle of my spiritual journey. This was new to me. I labored at writing out my reactions to others, evaluating why I felt the way I did, writing down questions I had about my future. I soon discovered the value of thinking with a pencil in my hand.

Dawson Trotman, founder of The Navigators, was right: "Thoughts untangle and make more sense as they pass through articulating finger-tips." A while ago, I saw a bumper sticker on a car paraphrasing this truth: "Don't believe every-thing you think!" When I started writing down what I was thinking and feeling, I could look at my thoughts more objectively and determine whether to believe them or discard them. Talk about getting the lead out!

I began to air out my head and empty my heart as I candidly processed the pain in my life. My roommates served as a valuable sounding board. A prayer-and-share group of students in my journaling class became a sort of surrogate family. I even sought the help of a Christian psy-chologist. But it was the discipline of making daily entries that lifted the overcast as I proceed-ed slowly through my soul's long, dark night.

The speed of my journey increased markedly when my professor gave us permission to start writing prayers in our journals. At first, that troubled me. The church I'd grown up in frowned at written prayers. I guess they seemed stilted and unspontaneous. But I decided to try writing out my prayers as letters to God. The more I did it, the more I experienced a tangible sense of God's presence as I wrote. Prayers of confession didn't just hang in midair; by writing down what I had done wrong, I knew I had come clean with the Lord. As I continued to "pray with a pencil," I probed the heart of God with hard questions I had about why bad things happen to Christians. I started goal setting in my journal. I created pro-and-con decision-making charts. Much to my surprise, I realized I was praying. After all, isn't prayer communicating the innermost concerns of your heart to the Lord? Well, that's what I was doing as I reflected and wrote.

> It was the discipline of making daily entries that lifted the overcast as I proceeded slowly through my soul's long, dark night.

Have you ever prayed that way? It's called praying with a pencil. It's a fascinating way to refresh your prayer life and a practical way to maintain the kind of regular contact with the Father that characterized Jesus' ministry. The first action step in the 50-Day Spiritual Adventure *Celebrate Jesus: Discovering What Makes Him Attractive to So Many People* is called "Pray with a Pencil."

How does it work? Set aside a time each day to talk with God—and grab a pencil and your Adventure Journal as you do. As you pray the "Show me Prayer" found in your journal, pause after each request to listen for what God might say. You may also want to add whatever specific question or need comes to mind.

Writing prayers and journaling my thoughts and feelings with the view that God was looking over my shoulder made me want to spend more time in his presence. I had a desire to be more alive to him and to life, and I knew a notebook and my No. 2 would serve me well. I even wrote a variation on a prayer I'd learned as a toddler to help me remember the power of keeping a prayer journal and the need to take responsibility for my life: "Now I sit me down to think and jot some notes with pen and ink. If I should wake before I die, I ask you Lord to help me try to live each day for what it's worth and make some meaning of my birth."

We have no record of Jesus writing anything (except using his finger to write in the dirt when the Pharisees dragged the adulterous woman to him). But we have ample evidence of the pattern he guarded of maintaining an intimate connection with the Father. What puts it all into perspective for me is recalling what the disciples asked the only time they requested Jesus teach them to do something. They didn't say, "Lord, teach us how to turn water into wine." They didn't entreat him to show them how to walk on water or raise the dead. Having observed his practice of remaining spiritually connected and directed, they asked, "Lord, teach us to pray" (Luke 11:1).

In spite of teaching his awestruck disciples the Lord's Prayer, the most important thing he taught them did not require words. Through his actions and predictable absences, he taught them how to stay spiritually connected and directed. The language he used was his life. As you read through the Gospels over the next 7 weeks, you'll discover that what we observed in Capernaum was not unique.

In fact, it is a pattern. Wherever Jesus went, people followed—and not just a few. Throughout the Gospels, we read how large crowds gathered. The atmosphere was electric. There was emotional static everywhere. Jesus was the cause. A power surge emanating from his healing hands touched people. Sick and disabled lives no longer limped to premature death dirges. Jesus gave them a new reason to wake up in the morning. He put a spring in their step. He put a glint in their eyes. They followed him wherever he went.

Like the old television commercial for E. F. Hutton, when Jesus spoke, people listened! They were all ears. As he taught them, they were dumbfounded. And as he healed the possessed and the blind, they were physically transformed. More than that, they became teachable.

That's my prayer for you, that you let the Teacher teach you. As you spend time in God's Word every day and get caught up in the fevered pitch of Jesus' up-front ministry, pay close attention to his practice of quiet solitude in the cool of the day as he consistently drank in his Father's presence.

For Discussion:

1. What impresses you about Jesus' sense of direction?

2. Whom do you know who models a pattern of personal Bible study and prayer? Is this a person you want to be more like?

3. What convictions (if any) do you hold as firmly as Eric Lidell's determination not to compete on Sundays?

4. How do you feel about Bonhoeffer's twin warnings (page 13)?

5. What pros or cons do you see to praying with a pencil? If you can, document your commitment to give this action step a try.

The Kingdom of Color

Oscar's a grouch!
No black and white entries
will be awarded any longer.
The kingdom of color has come.
The NBC peacock
is demanding center stage.
And for good reason.
There's splendor
in the spectrum.
All the shades are equal.
We are one.
Us is them!

—gea

CHAPTER
TWO

A Caste-less Cast of Characters

THREE FOOTBALL FIELDS LONG. Eleven stories tall. Ninety-two feet wide. She tipped the scales at 46,000 tons. She was the largest and most luxurious ship ever built. The pride of the White Star British shipping line was valued in 1912 currency at $7.5 million dollars. This ship fit for a king could carry nearly 3,000 passengers and crew. She had her own swimming pools, suites, restaurants, Turkish baths, and squash courts—even a Parisian sidewalk cafe (complete with strolling musicians). With 16 watertight compartments below sea level, she was deemed unsinkable. All 14,000 Irish workers at Harland and Wolfe Shipbuilders in Belfast took pride in the fact that she was the most seaworthy vessel ever constructed. They should have. It took them 36 months of painstaking effort.

I love the way Chuck Swindoll describes the *Titanic*'s unexpected demise.

> A mere five days into her romantic voyage, she was kidnapped and shortly thereafter killed by a cold, heartless iceberg lying in wait for her 350 miles southeast of Newfoundland. The rest is familiar albeit tragic history. . . . For nearly three-

quarters of a century, the grand old lady was celebrated in legend. Her skirt festooned by decades of decay and sediment. Her necklace tarnished and twisted. Though still impressive in her dimensions, her touch of elegance is gone. She is no longer the graceful maiden who slipped away on her first date. (*The Quest for Character,* copyright © 1982 by Charles R. Swindoll, Inc. Zondervan Publishing House, Grand Rapids, Mich., p. 11.)

Perhaps you've seen the 1998 fictional account of this sobering tale. The horrors graphically reenacted in James Cameron's blockbuster movie portray more than a sinking ship. You have a sinking feeling in your gut as you contemplate the names, faces, and families of all those 1,522 who perished and the 706 who were rescued.

Though fictionalized, this movie version of the *Titanic* tragedy was based on thousands of pages of factual investigations and historically accurate research. Those aboard the doomed ship represented an enormously broad spectrum of humanity. Wealthy businessmen, middle-class vacationers, dirt-poor immigrants, stowaways, crew. Young, old, those in between. The class distinction was not imaginary, and neither was the disproportional number of survivors. Sixty percent of those in first-class were saved. Forty-two percent of those in second-class survived. And only twenty-five percent of those in third class (and of the crew) lived to tell of their floating hell. There is something morally wrong with those statistics. Too many *haves* made it. Too many *have-nots* did not.

The diversity of passengers on the *Titanic* reminds me of the wide diversity there is in the body of Christ. People come in all flavors: rich, poor, and middle class. And we come in all colors. Remember that little song we learned as children? "Red and yellow, black and white, they are precious in his sight."

Unfortunately, not only is it beautifully diverse, the church of Jesus Christ is sadly divided. How many brands of Baptists are there? Not to mention Presbyterians, Methodists, Catholics, Nondenominationalists, Lutherans, Brethren, Episcopalians, Nazarenes, Adventists, Pentecostals, and scores of others. We disagree about baptism and Communion and the gifts of the Holy Spirit. We divide over the kinds of songs we sing, the style of the pastor's sermon, and whether our weekly worship is primarily for mature Christians or curious nonbelievers.

Jesus shattered the stereotypes of "us" and "them."

God's heart must be broken over the things that break us up. As my friend Dan likes to say, Jesus established one church, not a shopping mall of denominations. And yet we look like the self-serving castes of humanity on the *Titanic*. Keeping to ourselves, we're shocked when a wealthy high-society woman falls in love with a penniless gambler. Or when a nice Baptist boy falls in love with a girl whose doctrinal background raises parents' eyebrows. Or when an evangelical believer meets with a Catholic colleague at work for prayer and Bible study.

And it's not just in the church that we categorize people. Some fashion consultants have identified the four seasons of the year to distinguish the color of clothing people look best in.

I've been told I'm a Winter. My wife is a Spring. You may be a Summer or a Fall.

The Myers-Briggs personality profile codifies work styles and behavioral tendencies into a four-letter label. I'm an ENFP. But you probably already guessed that. Our children are issued grades by teachers who use those alphabetical designations as a way of separating the smart from the not-so-smart. Our driver's license indicates an *M* or an *F*. Our voter registration card signifies a *D* or an *R* or an *I*. Seasons, numbers, and letters represent the categories we are slotted into and tend to slot others.

Sometimes the slotting is as arbitrary as impersonal company policy. Did you hear about the fifteen-year-old boy in Chicago who was stabbed by a gang of high-school-age thugs and left in a pool of blood 30 feet from a hospital emergency room? The boy's friends tried to carry him to the hospital but weren't strong enough. They ran into the ER asking for help, but the hospital employees refused. According to the staff on duty, hospital code prevented them from leaving the hospital to treat anyone. Wow! Can you believe that? First century pharisaism is alive and well. Unfortunately, the fifteen-year-old boy is not. He died waiting for an ambulance to be dispatched.

Jesus broke with conventions of cultural categorization. He shattered stereotypes of "us" and "them." He saw every person as created in the image of God. He believed each person—no matter his or her income, color, status, education, or circumstance—was equal. He would have agreed with the winsome view American humorist Will Rogers took of the population at large: "There is no such thing as strangers. They are just friends I haven't met yet!"

Just think of the culturally acceptable categories Jesus disregarded. He esteemed children as worthy of his time, attention, and public affection. In fact, he even used children as the standard by which to measure admissibility into the Kingdom of God. He touched lepers. He ate with "sinners." He taught Gentiles. He included women in his band of followers. The disciples' three-and-a-half-year journey shadowing Jesus must have been quite a trip. They thought they knew who they were, but as they spent more time with Jesus, the labels they'd used all their lives began to peel off. It must have been confusing. This new vintage of kingdom wine required new containers, but it eliminated the need for "boxes."

Nowhere is Jesus' disregard for boxes more apparent than in the fourth chapter of John. While commuting to Galilee from Jerusalem, Jesus and the disciples looked for a rest stop. They were weary and famished. Jesus knew exactly where he wanted to go. He'd decided on a famous oasis—Jacob's well.

I'm sure his companions resisted Jesus' suggestion. And for good reason. Even though all Jewish children had grown up learning about this landmark in Hebrew history, most had never been there. That's because Jacob's well was in Samaria— off-limits for those purebred descendants of Abraham. Because of the racial and theological prejudice that existed between Samaritans and Jews, as well as between Jews and Samaritans, Jews traveling north or south through this part of Israel made a detour that cost them quite a few miles and quite a bit of time. It was like that part of town you steer around even if it means driving out of your way.

But Jesus opted to stop at this controversial

spot. The disciples headed off into town to grab some lunch, while Jesus engaged a Samaritan in conversation. Strike one! And get this: The Samaritan was not just a Samaritan—this Samaritan was a woman. Strike two! They talked politics, sex, and religion. Definitely strike three! But Jesus stayed in the batter's box. Remember, boxes don't matter to him. He engaged her in a depth of conversation this nameless woman had never known. She began to catch on to the fact that not only was this Jew willing to swim upstream against the tide of prejudice, he was a Jew that spoke with the authority of God.

When the disciples came back from shopping for lunch, they expressed amazement that Jesus wasn't playing by the rules. But curiously, according to verse 27, the disciples didn't embarrass themselves by challenging Jesus' actions. They just stood there with their mouths hanging open. Fortunately, their ears were open, too, and what Jesus was teaching them by example began to sink in.

And notice the open hearts of the Samaritans in town. When the woman at the well went back to her village and reported what had happened, her neighbors returned with her. Just think. Samaritans that despised Jews as much as Jews despised Samaritans were willing to go listen to a Jew. See what happens when the cycle of stereotypes is broken? The disciples swallowed their indignation. The Samaritans acknowledged their thirst.

Unfortunately, we are more comfortable living with boxes than Jesus is. There is a certain security that goes along with slotting people into categories. But it's a false security. It's the kind of comfort one feels sailing on a luxury liner with first-class accommodations, unaware that the ship you are on is headed toward an iceberg.

What's in a Name?

Speaking of ships, let me tell you of one that successfully navigated the Atlantic Ocean about the same time the *Titanic* sunk. It carried a fourteen-year-old boy hoping the heartache of leaving his family in Greece would be erased by the uninhibited opportunities he'd find in America.

Tears of joy filled Haralambos' eyes as his ship approached the harbor of New York City. A miniature silhouette on the horizon gradually became a colossal-sized image of a woman holding a torch. The seeds of imagination began to germinate in this young immigrant's heart. Though homesick and alone, he had reached his destination: a nation of people who were free to pursue whatever they dreamed possible. American. The very name celebrated this land of opportunity. Amer I CAN.

Within weeks, Haralambos discovered that the land of the free and the home of the brave was not the Garden of Eden. He soon realized that democracy did not preclude prejudice. Dark complexion and broken English were not a popular combination in 1912. In spite of his ready smile and willingness to work, he was marked as an outsider. The pain of rejection began to penetrate a heart already pining for the familiar coastline of the Mediterranean Sea.

Thinking that an American name might better his chances at acceptance, Haralambos surrendered his birthright on the altar of a judge's bench. With the slam of gavel, Haralambos Athanasios Asimakoupoulos became Harry Smith.

I know that story well. Harry was my grandfather. The family name was not reclaimed until I was a senior in high school. I wish I could say my grandfather's choice to change his name resulted in a change of circumstances. Unfortunately, it wasn't that easy. He still bore the brunt of misguided hate and arrogant pride.

There's a name for that injustice. It's called prejudice. It is the systematic way we slot people into stereotypes without even thinking about what we are doing. For both those who harbor it and those who are recipients of it, this kind of prejudice robs individuals of their dignity and minimizes their personhood.

Sadly, 11 to 12 o'clock on Sunday morning is still the most segregated hour of the week.

When most of us think of stereotypes, we think in terms of race. And for good reason. The inhumane mistreatment of African Americans, Native Americans, and other ethnic groups is not relegated to history books alone. For some, bigotry remains a "box" that has been rationalized away long enough. The health of the Body of Christ is undermined and her integrity is compromised when racism is tolerated. Sadly, 11 to 12 o'clock on Sunday morning is still the most segregated hour of the week. The Sunday school is the last school system in North America to be integrated. Christians from sea to shining sea gather with those most like themselves to worship the God of all classes, colors, and cultures and are blind to their tendency to slot people in categorical identities.

When I have put on my grandfather's shoes and walked in my mind through the alleys of rejection and fear he faced, I ache for that lonely fourteen-year-old boy. I get angry at those who put him down or called him up short. But then a still, small voice within me calls *me* up short and begins to point to the crevices of my heart where my premature judgments of others hide.

Recently, the Lord began to expose some of my unjustifiable attitudes toward overweight people. I caught myself making comments about the size of people I see at a game, at the mall, or in a restaurant. My attitude is not one of pity or empathy, but disgust. Here is a prejudice that doesn't make sense. After all, my grandmother (Harry's wife) was obese. Not to mention that when I was a child I struggled with my own weight. I even wore husky jeans! But as the Lord continued to probe, pride emerged as the basis of my bias: "Since I'm an overcomer, anyone can be if they really want to be." And since they haven't chosen to be, I tend to look down on them.

But the Lord rebukes my pride and prejudice. "Some, unlike you, are genetically predisposed to weight problems. Others are so far beyond their ideal weight, discouragement and lack of visible results is more of a problem than food. Still others are covering hurt and rejection you can't imagine with the joy of eating!" *Ouch, Lord, that smarts! If anyone should be more understanding and tolerant of victims of the "battle of the bulge" it should be someone like me. I've fought that war and I've been accepted by you in spite of my numerous imperfections.*

To be honest, before the Lord began probing, I didn't know I had a problem. But like the guy who exercised regularly and felt great, only to be tested and found to have clogged arteries leading to his heart, I am grateful the Lord is diagnosing my discriminatory tendencies. Although the procedure is a bit painful, it is worth it. Once I admit my subconscious orientation to categorizing people, the process of responding like Jesus did can begin. The same will be true for you.

To that end, why not take five minutes right now and work through the following checklist to identify some labels you might be using to slot others in boxes inside and outside the church:

★ I feel superior whenever I am around a
_____. *(Fill in the blank.)* (African American, Native American, Asian, Hispanic, Caucasian, Third World refugee, etc.)

★ I know God is no respecter of persons, but I'm glad I'm not going to be in the shoes of
_____ come Judgement Day. *(Fill in the blank.)* (The homeless, people with AIDS, alcoholics, homosexuals, drug users, prostitutes, TV evangelists, politicians, etc.)

★ When I follow my natural inclinations, I tend to avoid _____. *(Fill in the blank.)* (Children, teenagers, those divorced, the handicapped, the elderly, those who attend a church whose doctrines I question, those on welfare, overweight people, short people, etc.)

★ I have difficulty accepting _____ in places of leadership at work or at church. *(Fill in the blank.)* (Women, men, youth, those I believe to be less educated, people who haven't been Christians as long as I have, etc.)

★ Unless my son or daughter marries a
_____ I will be fit to be tied. *(Fill in the blank.)* (College graduate, lifelong Protestant

Christian, native of an English-speaking country, Republican, Democrat, Christian from my denomination or church background, person his or her own age, etc.)

What can you observe about yourself from the way you filled in the blanks? Are you surprised at your responses? Would you say you are more prone to lump people together in groups than to see them as individuals?

Light Your Street

If Jesus opened the eyes of his disciples to their stereotypes on a walk from Jerusalem to Jacob's well, maybe he desires to open our eyes to our stereotypes by walking through our neighborhood with us. Action Step 2 invites you to explore that possibility. "Light Your Street" is an invitation to become involved in a lighthouse of prayer.

What that means is to become aware of the names and faces and needs and hopes of those who live around you. Walk your neighborhood in an attitude of prayer, silently talking to the Lord about people you may not even know. Invite those you do know to join you to pray for concerns of your community, schools, or neighbors. Build bridges of friendship with those who live on your street so that you can begin to pray for them by name.

My wife, Wendy, and I are just beginning to light our street. We know our neighbors to the right and the left and the one across the street. But we have a way to go. I have started walking my block and praying quietly. I pray for Meli, whose husband died five years ago, leaving her with three teenage daughters. One of those girls recently had a child out of wedlock. I can't imagine the heartache and challenge Meli faces on a daily basis. I pray for Scott and Denise and their three preschool-age children, that they will come to know Jesus as more than a cultural icon whose influence they acknowledge on Easter Sunday and Christmas Eve. I pray for Don and Margaret and their children, who feel displaced from extended family, having just relocated from Michigan. For the woman down the street whose husband unexpectedly died of a brain aneurysm in a London hotel room while on a business trip. For others whom I recognize but cannot call by name. We haven't yet invited neighbors to join us to pray for our community, our local schools, and the needs of those who live in our subdivision, but we will.

When you decide to be a lighthouse of influence, your eyes become searchlights, scanning your neighborhood for those who need Jesus. You'll find them across your backyard or across the street. You don't have to look very far. Pray that the Lord will open your eyes and warm your heart to that person or persons he wants to love through you this week.

A friend of mine is the superintendent of Evangelical Covenant churches in California and Arizona. He teaches younger pastors under his care a simple prayer with which he has begun his day for the past 40 years: "Lord, I'm available. Please show me today who needs you the most." My friend claims that the Lord has answered that little prayer time and time again. The key, he says, is being restfully available and instantly obedient.

Plan to invite that family who just moved in down the street over for pizza. But don't quit there. Create a roster of doctors, dentists, and grocery stores that will help them transition into your community. Let them know where you go to church. But don't invite them right off. String them along a bit. Build a relationship on genuine friendship, not on artificial bait to simply reel them into some church function.

How about that friend at work who just found out her mother has Alzheimer's disease? Influencing your world with the love of Jesus can be as simple as finding an appropriate card at Hallmark and jotting a personal note. Then, inquire from time to time how it's going, not only with the mother, but with her. When it seems appropriate, and when you mean it, mention you've been praying for her family.

For that agnostic husband who never comes with his wife to church except on Christmas Eve or Easter, suggest that you go out to a first-run movie some weekend as couples. You pick the movie. Ask around and identify one that has spiritual overtones and would lead to interesting dialogue over dessert after the show. During dessert, don't just steer the conversation to the metaphors of the movie. Ask this guy what things in life interest him. Over the next few weeks, look for examples of his interest in the newspaper, magazines, or on the Internet. Your interest in his interest will communicate volumes! He may not be ready to spend more time in church, but he will most likely be drawn to spending time with someone who is genuinely interested in him.

Sound too intimidating? It's not, really. But here's an easy way to begin. Start today to prayerfully identify those pre-Christians in your sphere of influence you believe God wants to beam the light of his truth through you. The lighthouse strategy is simple. Prayer, care, and—eventually—share. Start by praying for people and their needs. Pray daily.

Once a month, find some tangible way to care for those on your list. Listen to their pain. Try to identify the unique suffering to which they are vulnerable. What challenges in life leave them feeling emotionally paralyzed?

The lighthouse strategy is simple. Prayer, care, and—eventually—share.

And then, when you feel the time is right, share with them what Christ has done in your life. Maybe you already know someone well enough to invite them to church with you some Sunday. Influencing our worlds takes time. It's hard work. It can be messy. It often is inconvenient. But it is thoroughly rewarding.

If you are part of a small group, why not identify creative ways you can individually or corporately influence your neighbors and colleagues with God's love? You know how easy it is for the focus of our small group Bible study and fellowship time to be oriented to our needs. That's not all bad. Such groups are a necessary means of growing in discipleship and community. But small groups that are only inwardly focused are not living up to their potential.

Steve Sjogren, in his excellent book *Conspiracy of Kindness,* cautions Christians in small groups from thinking too small:

> Every group is a potential lighthouse with the combined brilliance of each member's spiritual flashlight pointed into the spiritually darkened community. The powerful light of the Spirit of God in us has the capacity to shine far beyond itself. Groups which are not focusing outwardly

can easily end up shining those flash-
lights into the eyes of one another. That
can easily prove to be distracting if not
dangerous. (*Conspiracy of Kindness,* copyright © 1993 by Steve Sjogren. Published
by Servant Publications, Ann Arbor, MI,
p. 186.)

What made Jesus so attractive was that he
saw the beauty in others. He looked beyond the
external packaging—by which we tend to judge
another's abilities or value—to see the gifts waiting to be unwrapped.

The Great Equalizer

In Matthew 8, a Roman centurion came to Jesus
on behalf of his servant who was deathly ill.
Once again, Jesus surprised his onlookers by
treating this Gentile with the same courtesy and
respect as he would a fellow Jew.

Jesus didn't think, "Oh, here is a despicable
representative of Rome, that pagan empire ruled
by perverse Caesars who dominate the land of
God's chosen people." Quite to the contrary.
Jesus listened to the man's heart-wrenching
request and offered to walk with the soldier to
his home.

Once again, Jesus' response to the Gentile
centurion broke the cycle of stereotypical behavior. You would have expected the Roman authority to let Jesus walk with him to his barracks. But
he didn't. Even though he had a right to, the
centurion didn't act with an air of superiority at
all. Rather, he insisted that Jesus not trouble himself with a journey but simply speak the word of
healing. Amazing! Jesus shattered the stereotype
of how Jewish people related to Gentiles, and, in

turn, the Gentile in question shattered the stereotype of how Roman officers responded to Jewish rabbis. The ground on which these two men stood was level. Call it mutual respect. Call it personal interaction. Call it life without boxes! The clincher is this: Jesus turned to his true blue Jewish purebred disciples and said this Gentile's faith put theirs to shame. Whoa, Nellie! I think they got knocked off their high horses.

I have a friend by the name of Red. I know he knows the Lord. He loves God with all his heart. But that's not all he loves. Red's carried a secret for a long, long time. Even though he's been a popular Sunday school teacher and an active churchman, Red is a closet alcoholic. His life has recently crumbled around him. His wife divorced him. He lost his job. He was arrested twice in the same week for driving under the influence. As a result, he's lost his driver's license for two years. Looking up from the bottom of a well as deep as Jacob's, Red is starting all over on most levels of his life. He is in counseling. He's in a spiritual accountability group. He is religiously working the 12 steps of Alcoholics Anonymous.

> **We are all in recovery from a chronic spiritual sickness called sin. The ground is level. There is no room for pride.**

Red told me the other day what an equalizing experience an AA meeting is. Everybody introduces himself or herself the same way. Whether you've been sober for 10 years or 10 days, you say "Hi, my name is _____, and I'm an alcoholic!" It occurred to me what a powerful symbol that is of everybody in the church and everybody in the world. We are all in recovery from a chronic spiritual sickness called sin. The ground is level. There is no room for pride. "Hi, my name is _____, and I'm a sinner." That's what Jesus was trying to tell us.

At the very end of *Titanic,* there is a scene that goes by so fast, most people miss its significance. There, on the opulent circular staircase beneath the crystal chandelier, is a gathering of all those individuals we met in the course of the film. It is a picture of those who died. The rich, the poor, the middle class. Passengers, crew, stowaways. The director seems to be making a statement. If death is the great equalizer, why can't life be as well?

For Jesus, love was the great equalizer. By his loving disposition toward everyone, he shattered stereotypes of the *haves* and the *have-nots*, of the wealthy and the poor, of "us" and "them."

There is a curious sidebar in the actual records of the *Titanic* disaster. Of those who perished on the *Titanic* was John Jacob Astor, one of the wealthiest men in America. His pregnant wife, Madeleine, was rescued. Upon reaching New York, she discovered that Astor's will had bequeathed her the income from his five-million-dollar trust fund and the use of his homes on Fifth Avenue and in Newport, Rhode Island. There was a catch, however. You guessed it! Madeleine would have to forfeit the entire fortune if she ever remarried. Four months after the *Titanic* sank, she gave birth to a son and named him after her deceased husband. Within five years, she fell in love and married William K. Dick. Following her heart, Madeleine Astor willingly relinquished her inheritance. Love matters more than wealth.

And Jesus would add, love matters more than

any other category we devise to separate ourselves from other people. Love is the great equalizer. It is also the power that enables us to light our street and our world.

> I'll be a lighthouse, guiding lives to Jesus.
> Lost ships at sea for which the Savior died.
> Unanchored souls known by first names
>   and faces,
> with fragile egos, anxious hopes, and pride.
> A world unreached with knowledge of
>   salvation.
> A generation I've been called to serve.
>
> I'll bring my world to Christ through acts
>   of friendship.
> A listening ear, a hand that reaches out.
> Making the time to get to know my
>   neighbors.
> Discovering their passions, fears, and
>   doubts.
> Extending mercy when their hearts are
>   broken.
> Transparently acknowledging my pain.
>
> I'll bring my world to Christ, convinced
>   he'll use me.
> Just as I am, I'm a partner in his plan.
> I'll choose to be the salt and light he's
>   called me,
> creating thirst for God in this dark land.
> I'll bring my world to Christ, anticipating
> the varied ways he'll choose to answer
>   prayer.

—*gea*

For Discussion:

1. What mental stereotypes did you inherit, growing up in your family?

2. What progress have you made in your attempts not to slot people in categories but rather view them as individuals?

3. What is there about Jesus' interaction with the woman at the well that intrigues you? Explain.

4. Explain as best you can how one person's unexpected response can break the cycle of prejudice.

On Kissing Frogs

Warts didn't cause him
to keep his distance.
He was the original frog-kisser.
He refused to jump to conclusions
about the status quo.
But, he sure could leap in his mind
to see how the future would find
these unlovable frogs.
And because of his kiss
and his loving embrace,
he saw princes with crowns
and princesses in lace.

—gea

CHAPTER
THREE

The Pro-People Protagonist

IT HAD BEEN AN EXHAUSTING SATURDAY. My wife and I had just dropped into bed to watch a favorite television show before turning out the lights. A news bulletin interrupted our program. "Princess Diana and her male companion were involved in a car accident in Paris. Authorities report that Dodi Al-Fayed was killed. The Princess of Wales is hospitalized in serious condition." As the news anchor returned us to our regularly scheduled programming, something stirred inside me. I turned to Wendy and said, "I think Diana is dead, too! I bet they are just delaying the announcement."

Within the hour, another news flash confirmed my intuition. Princess Di and Dodi had both been killed. Over the next 48 hours, television cameras captured the reaction of a world in mourning. An unprecedented outpouring of sympathy saturated the airwaves. No one could deny that the Queen of Hearts was loved by humanity. For the next few days, a planet of six billion people didn't seem so huge. The death of one individual drew us together, if only emotionally.

Less than a week later, another woman, equally as famous, died. Mother Teresa of Calcutta had succumbed to heart failure at the age of eighty-seven.

A heart that had carried the hurt of the diseased and dying for more than half a century wore out. Once again, the world seemed strangely unified as reporters converged on Calcutta, and we felt like we'd lost a favorite great aunt. Even though the televised coverage of Mother Teresa's funeral was not nearly as extensive as that of Princess Di's, the media did provide us with a window through which we were able to witness a Hindu nation pay its last respects to a deeply loved Catholic nun.

As I reflected on the passing of these two celebrated individuals, I had a flash of insight. No two women could have been more different. One, dwarfed in stature and withered by age, preached grace. The other, tall and graceful, was the epitome of youthful beauty. Her materialistic lifestyle was a message without need for words. One died a pauper, the other a millionaire. But Teresa and Diana shared one thing in common: Both of them were moved with compassion to the needs of the poor, the maimed, the ostracized, and the homeless. Both of them responded in love and stooped to touch the untouchables of society. And that is why the world grieved their deaths with unprecedented adulation. Both women distinguished themselves as heroines through their unconditional love of humanity.

Then it dawned on me. What we loved about these women were the qualities of Jesus we observed in them. The reasons we were attracted to Mother Teresa and Princess Diana were some of the same reasons those who followed Jesus around the Judean countryside were attracted to him: He liked people and drew out the best in them, no matter their station in life.

In 1972, a movie was made based on Cervantes's timeless epic, *Don Quixote*. The plot is about a middle-aged landowner who imagines himself a knight in armor and goes into the world of the sixteenth century to battle injustice. The musical film version was called *The Man of La Mancha.* I don't know about you, but I was never sure if the bearded knight on a tired horse was playing with a full deck or not. Certainly he needed glasses. He saw in windmills enemies to be engaged in battle. Foolishly, he came at the rotating blades attempting to joust them. He was a lone lancer who galloped to his own cadence and saw what others could not.

But his abnormal perception was not entirely out of touch with reality. In a disheveled and hardened "woman of the night," he saw a prisoner of men's lust, longing to be freed. Her name was Aldonza. But Don Quixote didn't see in her what others noticed. He saw a beautiful girl with a story still being written. He referred to her as "My Lady." He gave her a new name—Dulcinea. And in one of the more poignant passages in the film, he sings of her new name.

If you cannot see a Christ-figure in Don Quixote, maybe *you* need glasses. No doubt the writer was drawing on his knowledge of Christianity when he wove his plot around the Don and Dulcinea. What a remarkable parallel there is in this story by Cervantes and the episode in the life of Jesus in which the adulteress woman was dragged from her worn-out mattress into his presence (John 8:1–11). The religious leaders saw one thing. Jesus saw another. In forgiving her, he renamed her. No longer guilty, she was now clean. Jesus loved her—in the true sense—and drew out the best in her.

He gave his disciple Simon a new name and a new purpose in life. He chose to call the flighty fisherman, who suffered from foot-in-the-mouth disease, *Peter*. That new name meant "the Rock." Even though Jesus was, no doubt, bothered by the sandal tracks on Peter's tongue, he liked the burly fisherman. He liked his honesty. He liked his bravado. Jesus saw in Simon's brash confidence a quality of unrefined strength. By calling him a rock, Jesus didn't hold up a mirror; rather, he painted a vision. He held before Peter a picture of a preferred future. Jesus saw what no one else could see. He saw in the tomorrows to come how that unhewn boldness would be sculpted into a boulder of strength. He perceived a strong leader who would anchor the faith of the other disciples. He saw in Peter one whose love of the "catch" would be best utilized casting for perishing people instead of perch. So he fashioned a future for Peter that served as a magnet. From that fateful day on, Peter was drawn to become the man with a mission Jesus envisioned.

Jesus liked people and drew out the best in them.

It happened again—with Zacchaeus and Nicodemus and Mary Magdalene—and over and over again. Jesus liked people and drew out the best in them. His predisposition to bring home the underdogs and not leave them out on the streets bespoke his belief in their worth.

Take Matthew the tax collector. Not the most enviable person in town. The Jews saw him as a traitor. They saw all tax collectors that way. These "despicable" men had sold out to the Romans. You see, they not only collected exorbitant taxes, but they added on whatever they thought they could get away with to feather their own finan-

cial nests. In fact, if you read the Gospels carefully, you can see that *tax collectors* and *sinners* are
used synonymously.

It's safe to assume that Matthew knew he had
enemies. He'd heard the expletives fall from the
lips of those who deposited their coins in his rev-
enue box and withdrew in angered haste. Matthew
knew he was despised, but perhaps he didn't have
much choice. It was a paying job. At least he had
friends—the other tax collectors. Still, it must have
been a dreaded existence. No matter the payoff,
cold, hard cash doesn't warm a lonely heart.

It is into this lonely life that Jesus peered and
saw a treasure to be mined. To that end, he broke
with tradition and rewrote the rules for relating to
people of Matthew's kind. Curiously, it is in chapter 9 that Matthew later recorded Jesus' break with
traditional norms. Jesus approached this sinner
with a smile and a handshake. He didn't see a
hated man doomed to spend the rest of his life
writing in a debit book and deflecting vicious
stares. He saw a man who had the ability to use
his pen to preserve the Good News of a kingdom
whose time had come. Matthew responded to
Jesus' overture of friendship by throwing a party
and inviting his colleagues to meet his new friend.
It was a veritable tax collectors' convention.

Jesus didn't appear to be uncomfortable with
the setting; in fact, he rather enjoyed himself. I
can imagine him laughing and telling stories. His
love for people is not conditioned on their spiritual sensitivity. He just likes people. And from that
day on, two things are true: Matthew became
known as a disciple of Jesus, and Jesus became
known as a friend of sinners. As such a friend, he
remains The People's Choice.

An Embrace of Acceptance

While watching the news coverage surrounding the search for John F. Kennedy, Jr.'s missing plane, I recalled an earlier episode involving this famous American family. I remembered watching the election returns of the California presidential primary on our black-and-white television. It was a warm June evening in 1968. My parents and my brother had gone to bed. As a high schooler, I was intrigued by the political process and stayed up past midnight to watch Senator Robert F. Kennedy make his victory speech. What followed a few minutes later has remained etched in my memory. The eerie sight of a wounded Bobby Kennedy lying face up, eyes open, dying. A few days later, on the same black-and-white TV, I watched the funeral service. The only surviving Kennedy brother eulogized the slain candidate. I can still hear Teddy Kennedy's quivering voice verbalizing his older brother's optimism. "Some men see things as they are and ask why. Bobby saw things as they might be and asked, 'Why not?'"

Whether you classify yourself as a Kennedy Democrat, a Reagan Republican, or something in-between, you have to admit that Bobby Kennedy's determination to celebrate the potential of a person or a cause was nothing less than what Jesus modeled. The Son of God knew that all have sinned and fallen short of God's glory. But he resisted easy answers. He refused to simply define human beings as morally depraved. In spite of how they tend to behave, he gave them reason to believe that they could become what God intended them to be.

The Pharisees and scribes did the finger-pointing, asking, "Why are you like you are?" Jesus reached his arm around the stooped shoulders of those already aware of their sin and asked, "Why not believe that all things are possible—even a fresh start?" Mark Twain is credited with having said, "There's only eighteen inches difference between a swat on the rear and a pat on the back, but miles separate the results." One judges the less-than-desirable present, the other motivates a possible future. The legalistic teachers of the law would not have been known as liking people. By contrast, Jesus did. And his embrace of acceptance made all the difference in the world.

Have you ever been relationally embraced by someone who believed in you when you doubted your worth? I have. John was the conference superintendent when I served my first church out of seminary. He regularly wrote me notes and called on the phone to check up on me. He knew my tendency toward discouragement and consistently looked for ways to praise me. One day in particular comes to mind.

I was leading worship for a retreat of several hundred people at our church conference center in the Santa Cruz mountains. We were gathered in an outdoor amphitheater on a warm summer morning in the shadow of giant California redwood trees. As I led the people in prayer, I thanked the Lord for the beauty of his creation. I took care to paint word pictures that would provide those gathered in worship a vocabulary of praise. At the end of the service, John came up to me and said, "Greg, you're a pastor with a poet's heart."

A light turned on inside me. Someone I deeply respected had called me by a name no one had used before. The name he bestowed on me gave me permission to pursue and develop a gift that had been buried for years. Since that time, I have celebrated my gift of artistic language. I have written poetry to comfort those dealing with disease, death, divorce, and depression. My poems that have celebrated life and joy have been published. Poetry and hymn-writing have become an intrinsic part of my ministry. And all because John Notehelfer took time to celebrate me.

John celebrated people because, as a young immigrant child in the '40s, others had befriended and drawn out the best in him. Born in Japan of German missionaries, John and his family were forced to flee during World War II. They settled in the little Swedish village of Turlock, California, where immigrants knew how to care for immigrants. John and his siblings and parents had an accent, but so did most everybody else at the Mission Covenant Church. It was the church that reached out in love the way others had reached out to them years before. As a result, wonderful things took place. Young John became a pastor. So did two of his brothers. And one of his sisters married a pastor. All are gifted in the art of friendship and encouragement. They are living examples of what happens when we emulate Jesus' example of drawing out the best in people.

Loving the Lost

I'm convinced Jesus' approach to people is as attractive as ever. Whenever the world gets a glimpse of his unconditional love, acceptance, and forgiveness, it stands on tiptoe for an unrestricted view. You see, I believe non-Christians have a lot more interest in Jesus than we might think. Those who are aware of their sin, and the broken hearts and broken dreams that result from their sin, don't tend to have a problem with Jesus but with his Bride. I heard it put this way once: "The world doesn't have difficulty with

Jesus. It's his wife they struggle with liking."
That's right. The church and the people who
make up the church are often what keep non-
Christians away.

And there's a good reason. For the most part,
we have not done a very good job emulating
Jesus when it comes to liking people. Oh yes,
we've learned how to say, "We hate the sin but
love the sinner." Still, when it comes to genuinely loving people caught in the cycle of self-
destructive or unattractive lifestyles, we don't
deserve a passing grade.

We're offended by those who look different,
act differently, smell different, or vote differently
than we do. We don't have time for someone
who has been married three times and is current-
ly living with a lover. We tend to look down our
noses at someone who smells of smoke or alcohol or body odor. We have trouble being courte-
ous to a homosexual. Those dressed in shabby
clothes conjure up suspicion of welfare fraud.
Feelings of hate begin to bubble to the surface
when someone articulates a pro-choice position
on abortion. How many disciples of Jesus in your
church would be comfortable being called a
friend of sinners?

Dwight L. Moody was a nineteenth-century
shoe salesman in Chicago who became an effective pastor. No one who knew him would doubt
that Moody had the heart of an evangelist. What
I mean is, he loved Christians—but he loved
non-Christians more. He channeled his energies
in order to draw people to Christ. Just recently, I
was in the church Moody founded. It is a beautiful edifice whose immense size testifies to the
founder's vision to reach the unchurched. It was
a vision grounded in loving the lost.

According to Moody, "The churches would soon be filled if outsiders could find that people in them loved them when they came. This . . . draws sinners! We must win them to us first, then we can win them to Christ" (*Too Soon to Quit,* copyright © 1999 by George Sweeting. Moody Press, Chicago, p. 35).

Moody had the heart of an evangelist. He loved Christians—but he loved non-Christians more.

Maybe it is possible to love people we do not *like* in some broad theological definition of the word. I doubt it. So do those who feel held at arm's length by those who hang around the church. The Matthews of our world can detect the difference between tolerance and acceptance a mile away.

In the last church I pastored, I articulated a vision for ministry that basically said, "The church is the only institution that exists primarily for the sake of those who are not yet its members. We are not meant to be an equipping center as much as we are called to be a mission outpost on a secular frontier." I strongly believe that. One Monday night, as the elders gathered to evaluate the programs and ministries of our congregation, I had the wind knocked out of my sails. One of the more influential members of the board publicly challenged my vision. He said it was unbiblical. I was devastated. Within a few months I was without a job.

If my read of the ecclesiastical landscape is correct, there will be an increasing number of pastors out of a job. Some, like me, will be displaced by congregations more concerned with being a church of friends than a friendly church. But others will be sent packing because their church has died. Believe it or not, churches are locking their doors at an alarming rate. According to researcher George Barna, while three churches are started each day in North America, twenty go out of business for good.

The trend will, no doubt, continue unless local congregations, and the Christians that compose them, recapture their mission. Rescuing lost people who do not have a moral compass or a spiritual anchor, who are helplessly adrift on the dangerous coastline of a godless culture, is the calling of every congregation. Those who worship The People's Choice every week can't ignore the fact that his choice was to spend his public ministry in one continuous search-and-rescue mission. Thanks to Mission America, we are being reminded of how to function as lighthouses for the lost.

The Story of the Lifesaving Station

Theodore Wedel tells the story of the lifesaving station. You've probably heard it before, but it bears considering again. It is a powerful little parable that reminds us what we are to be about as followers of One whose heart broke for the broken and lost.

On a dangerous seacoast where shipwrecks often occur, there was once a crude little lifesaving station. The building was just a hut, and there was only one boat, but the few devoted members kept a constant watch over the sea and, with no thought for themselves, went out day and night, tirelessly searching for the lost. Some of those who were saved, and various others in the surrounding area, wanted to become associated with the station and give of their time and money and effort for the support of its work. New boats were bought and new crews trained. The little lifesaving station grew.

Some members of the lifesaving station were unhappy that the building was so crude and poorly equipped. They felt that a more comfortable place should be provided as the first refuge of those saved from the sea. They replaced the emergency cots with beds and put better furniture in the enlarged building.

Now the lifesaving station became a popular gathering place for its members, and they decorated it beautifully and furnished it exquisitely, because they used it as a sort of club. Fewer members were now interested in going to sea on lifesaving missions, so they hired lifeboat crews to do this work. The lifesaving motif still prevailed in this club's decorations, and there was a miniature lifeboat in the room where the club initiations were held.

About this time, a large ship was wrecked off the coast, and the hired crews brought in boatloads of cold, wet, and half-drowned people. They were dirty and sick and some of them had black skin and some had yellow skin. The beautiful new club was in chaos. So the property committee immediately had a shower house built outside the club where victims of the shipwreck could be cleaned up before coming inside.

At the next meeting, there was a split in the club membership. Most of the members wanted to stop the club's lifesaving activities as being unpleasant and a hindrance to the normal social life of the club. Some members insisted upon lifesaving as their primary purpose and pointed out that they were still called a lifesaving station. But

they were finally voted down and told that if
they wanted to save the lives of all the various
kinds of people who were shipwrecked in those
waters, they could begin their own lifesaving station down the coast. They did.

> **Some members insisted upon life-
> saving as their primary purpose.
> But they were finally voted down.**

As the years went by, the new station experienced the same changes that had occurred in the
old. It evolved into a club, and yet another lifesaving station was founded. History continued to
repeat itself, and if you visit that seacoast today,
you will find a number of exclusive clubs along
the shore. Shipwrecks are frequent in those
waters, but most of the people drown.

Can we see lost people the way Jesus sees
them? Sure, they are sinful—but likeable. True,
they are misguided—but pregnant with a God-
planted potential that longs to be reached and
released. If Jesus liked people and drew out the
best in them, can we as his church do any less?

I play and play and never tire of a song we
have on a CD at home. The haunting words of
"Not Too Far From Here" are a continual
reminder of my purpose as a follower of Jesus:

> Somebody's down to their last dime
> Somebody's running out of time
> Not too far from here
> Somebody's got nowhere else to go
> Somebody needs a little hope
> Not too far from here
> And I may not know their name
> But I'm praying just the same

That you'll use me, Lord
To wipe away the tears . . .

Now I'm letting down my guard
And I'm opening my heart
Help me speak Your love
To ev-'ry needful ear
Someone is waiting
Not too far from here

*(Text and music by Ty Lacy and Steve Siler,
© 1994 Shepherd's Fold Music, BMI/Ariose
Music.)*

The attitude we, as congregations, project
toward people will be the result of how we, as individual followers of Jesus, reach out in friendship
and concern to know those not too far from us. It
all comes down to recognizing the worth God has
birthed in human beings, no matter their skin
color, tax bracket, marital status, or how healthy
they are emotionally, physically, or spiritually.

Every person on this globe of ours was created in God's image. Everybody claims the divine
tattoo. Born in sin and shaped in iniquity? Yes,
but that's only part of the story. They are loved
by a God who longs to release the potential he's
planted in them. No wonder Jesus risked social
rejection to express friendship to people the religious leaders shunned. No wonder those who
recognized his sincere overture of unconditional
love were magnetically attracted to him.

Celebrate People

If we are going to celebrate Jesus and align our
actions with his attitude toward others, we'd better learn how to celebrate people. That's what

Jesus did. Action Step 3 in the 50-Day Spiritual Adventure invites us to do the same. It's a daily experiment in drawing near people in an attempt to bring out the God-implanted destiny he desperately wants them to own.

Every day, say something affirming to someone else. Thank them. Compliment them. Inspire them by commenting on some area of potential they exhibit. Celebrate who they are or whom they can become. You'll probably start with family and close friends, but eventually you'll reach out to affirm the kid at the corner store, the FedEx carrier, the checkout lady at Wal-Mart. Look for people of different ages, from children to senior citizens. It'll be fun to find new people to pay compliments to—and it will start to change your attitude.

With some people you don't know well, you might just applaud how they look or what they're wearing—but try to get beyond those surface things. Learn to look at people through the eyes of Jesus. You might say, "You have such a great smile. You seem to have a lot of joy in your life." Or, "I appreciate how well you do your job. It must be meaningful for you." You never know when positive comments like those might lead to life-changing conversations.

I can't imagine Jesus ignoring people, can you? Even if he was late for an appointment with his disciples and was walking at a fast gait down a dirt path, if he passed someone, I'm sure he at least smiled and said hello. I don't always do that. Do you?

Lately, I have spent a lot of time on airplanes, traveling the country introducing pastors and church leaders to the 50-Day Spiritual Adventure. More often than not, I am seated next to someone I do not know. I'm not proud to admit that my tendency (if I'm extremely tired) is to not even make eye contact, and I bury my nose in a book.

The Holy Spirit began to nudge me and challenge my self-focused agenda. The more I thought about it, the more I realized that Jesus would never be guilty of giving someone the silent treatment, unless that person made it clear he or she did not want to be greeted. For Jesus, every chance meeting was a never-to-be-repeated opportunity to celebrate the gift of friendship. Not that he would delve into the depths of theology with every person, but he would at least engage them in conversation and convey affirmation that would cause each one to feel special. I have so much to learn in that area.

What is more, Jesus would not be put off by those persons I have met in airplanes, airports, taxi cabs, and hotel lobbies whose body odor or stinky personalities are too unpleasant to contend with. Even when he had to breathe through his mouth, Jesus overlooked odors to find the attractive fragrance he detected down the road. Fortunately, I am making progress.

A Heart Beating for Hurting People

Let me introduce you to someone who has taught me how to look beyond the unattractiveness of people's lives and see the potential within them. Like her Lord, Bette Lou Benzinger genuinely likes people and brings out the best in them.

Her nameplate caught my attention. As you might expect, I have an appreciation for unusual last names. In all my previous trips to the bank, I had not recalled seeing her name at the cashier's window. She smiled to indicate it was my turn to approach the counter.

As I stepped forward and handed her my

deposit slip, she made a comment about my name. (We who have more than eight letters in our last name play that game.) She noticed the "Reverend" that preceded my first name and asked what church I pastored. Our conversation was brief but warm. As I turned to leave, I thanked her for her personal attention. Her face creased into the same engaging smile that had welcomed me a few minutes earlier. I didn't know it at the time, but it was a smile I would come to appreciate for years to come.

Although I never saw Bette Lou at the bank again, three months later I saw her smile in the congregation as I stood at the pulpit beginning my sermon. She greeted me at the door after worship. "I liked the service. You're a good preacher! I'll be back."

As was our custom at our church, first-time worshippers received a follow-up, personal visit. Our visitation team divided up contact cards and set out two by two with our weekly house calls. Laurie Dender and I were given Bette Lou's card.

The visit was a memorable one: upbeat, comfortable. Small talk wasn't necessary. Bette Lou had learned the art of conversation from her many years of welcoming customers in the bank. Our Evangelism Explosion questions weren't necessary either. Bette Lou was a mature Christian with a contagious faith. What wasn't so obvious was the emotional pain she had learned to successfully mask. Behind her signature smile was a story of incredible hurt.

As the evening wore on, the mask came off. Bette Lou was a survivor. After 35 years of marriage to an abusive alcoholic, she was barely able to hold her life together. With their six children grown and gone, so was the buffer zone a house full of other people provided. Bette Lou had recognized how vulnerable she was. As a Christian, she didn't believe in divorce, but her emotional and physical health was in jeopardy. If she were to have a life of her own, she'd have to make one for herself.

She arranged with friends from her old church to move out all her clothes and furniture while her husband was at work. When he arrived home that night, Bette Lou was gone. So were all of her personal effects. Intentionally, she left no trace of her whereabouts. Bette Lou knew that if her new location were discovered, her husband would take out his anger on her.

All the while, Bette Lou struggled with her decision to move out on Harold. She really did love him. There had been good times. They had been through a lot together, including a move from Chicago to California. She longed for him to trust Christ as his Savior. Still, she knew she couldn't remain a passive victim. Her children were divided about her actions. Some sided with their dad and openly criticized Bette Lou, which only increased her already intolerable emotional pain.

As Bette Lou continued to tell her story, it became obvious to Laurie and me that the home in which we were sitting was the secret hiding place she and one of her grown daughters were temporarily renting. She cautioned us not to give out the address to anyone. We promised. After a rich time of prayer, we said goodbye. Once again, that smile I first saw at the bank lit our way as we walked to the car.

Because our church was close to her "house of refuge," Bette Lou began attending on a regular basis. She told me she and Harold were seeing a counselor. He still didn't know where she was

living; they only met at the counselor's office.
Bette Lou was cautiously optimistic about reconciliation but reported that Harold was still upset
at being abandoned. He was still drinking.

> **One afternoon the phone rang. It
> was Bette Lou. The quiver in her
> voice indicated a problem.**

One afternoon while I was preparing my sermon, the phone rang. It was Bette Lou. The quiver
in her voice indicated a problem. "Harold was
found dead this morning," she blurted out. "The
doctors suspect it was a severe case of hepatitis!"

The hoped-for reconciliation would never be.
So many loose ends would forever be untied. As I
walked through the valley of death's shadow with
her and her children in preparation for the funeral, I realized how deeply broken Bette Lou was.
Her tears spoke volumes. They revealed the depth
of her love for a man who loved his bottle more.

Still, her ability to smile in the midst of her
pain spoke louder than her tears. It convinced
me that here was a godly woman who would not
let her pain be wasted. On her journey through
the wilderness of abuse, rejection, deception, and
codependency, she had learned how to survive.
She was determined to share those lessons with
anyone willing to learn.

During her difficult marriage, Bette Lou
became introduced to Al-Anon, a support group
based on the 12 steps of Alcoholics Anonymous
for family members of those who abuse alcohol
or drugs. She was encouraged by the fact we had
an Al-Anon group that met at our church on
Thursday nights. As she became more involved at
the church and acquainted with others in dys-

functional marriages, she invited them to attend the weekly meetings.

Bette Lou also invited me to open my eyes to the pain in my congregation. She could tell that I had developed skills in overlooking non-verbalized struggles. She offered me books to read on the 12 Step Movement. (I discovered this phenomenal program was based on Christian principles and began in a church.) Together, we attended seminars on recovery issues. My preaching began to reflect what Bette Lou was helping me learn.

I could see in Bette Lou a broken heart that beat for hurting people whose plight in life reflected hers. In our congregation, she befriended single women and those who came to worship alone because of unbelieving spouses. All the while, Bette Lou continued to validate the redemptive truths of the 12 Steps of AA as she painfully processed reconciliation with her children. Here was a woman committed to addressing pain wherever she encountered it, at home or at church. "You don't do anybody any good when you simply pretend there's no pain!" she would say.

One day she asked me why we couldn't offer a Sunday morning class that would provide the same kind of safe, honest sharing that the Al-Anon group provided on Thursday nights. I didn't have a good answer. Neither did the church council. And so, the Steppers Class was born.

It was a revolutionary idea in adult Sunday school. With Bette Lou as the facilitator, the Steppers met behind a closed door in my office during the education hour. They used a workbook from the local Christian bookstore that incorporated Scripture into the 12 Step framework. Hurts were shared, stories told, prayers offered. Everything was confidential. Nothing was out of bounds, except comments that judged another. The popularity of the class led to the creation of another.

Soon after the second class was added, Bette Lou and I met over lunch. She smiled as she reported on the attendance at the unorthodox adult classes. My heart smiled as I realized what was transpiring. Here before my eyes was the living out of 2 Corinthians 1:3–4: "Praise be to the God and Father of our Lord Jesus Christ, the Father of compassion and the God of all comfort, who comforts us in all our troubles, so that we can comfort those in any trouble with the comfort we ourselves have received from God."

> **"Praise be to the God . . . who comforts us in all our troubles, so that we can comfort those in any trouble" (2 Corinthians 1:3–4).**

This woman, whose life had been crushed by the crippling weight of alcohol abuse, had not only tasted the comfort of God's intoxicating grace, but she had also found a tangible way to slake the thirst of those who longed for acceptance, understanding, and encouragement in hard situations. In his book *The Wounded Healer,* the late Henri Nouwen described those who minister out of their imperfect past. In Bette Lou Benzinger, I saw this reality illustrated in living color.

About this time, Bette Lou realized that with her husband's death benefits and her accumulated pension from the bank, she could take an early retirement. As we met at Starbucks over a cup of French roast, Bette Lou remarked that she would like to channel more of her time and energy into the ministries of our church.

This time, it was my turn to smile. I asked her if she might consider coming on staff at the church as Director of Recovery Ministries. She responded enthusiastically. Not being able to pay her a salary was no obstacle—she didn't need additional income. All she desired was an opportunity to continue to develop a ministry that no church in our area had ever attempted. We weren't sure what the job description should be but decided that it would be okay to let it evolve.

And evolve it did. The two support groups on Sunday morning grew to four, including one for youth and one for men. Under Bette Lou's leadership, an Alcoholics Anonymous group began using our facilities on Monday nights, in addition to the Al-Anon group on Thursdays. The old ranch house on the church property, which had been used for children's Sunday school, became Recovery House. Bette Lou set up an office in it and created a library of books that related to personal growth, Christian psychology, and discipleship. Having completed an accredited course in lay counseling, Bette Lou was a natural to shoulder the increasing load of pastoral care and visitation. Her empathy and listening techniques proved invaluable as I assigned counseling opportunities to her.

Countless women in crisis have been cared for by this retired bank teller. More than a few marriages have been saved through her tireless efforts and prayerful ministry. And her abilities became known beyond the boundaries of our church. The planning committee of the San Francisco Bay Area Sunday School Convention asked if she would teach an annual workshop on starting a recovery ministry in the local church.

It's been over 10 years since Bette Lou first flashed a smile at me in the lobby of Bank of America. It's been over four years since our family left California for Chicago. But Bette Lou Benzinger continues to serve as Director of Recovery Ministries, long after many women her age have hung up their business suits. And she's still serving others with a smile.

In the unforgettable plot of *The Man of La Mancha,* Don Quixote drew out the best in a prostitute's life and laid to rest the less-than-best. The lyrics of his song of redemption, "Dulcinea," still ring in my ears, but so do the words of a song more people recognize. The heart of Don Quixote is laid wide open in "The Impossible Dream":

To dream the impossible dream.
To fight the unbeatable foe.
To bear with unbearable sorrow.
To run where the brave dare not go.
To right the unrightable wrong.
To love pure and chaste from afar.
To try when your arms are too weary.
To reach the unreachable star.

This is my quest. To follow that star.
No matter how hopeless. No matter how
    far.
To fight for the right, without question or
    pause.
To be willing to march into Hell for a
    heavenly cause.

(Joe Darion, copyright © 1968 by Andrew Scott, Inc. Hal Leonard Corp., Milwaukee, Wis.)

It's a song I can imagine Mother Teresa humming as she spooned cereal to a dying child. It's a song I can hear Princess Diana whistling as she walked the hospital corridor en route to visit civilians maimed by detonated mines.

Frankly, had it been written back then, I can visualize Jesus singing it in full voice as he made his final trek from Capernaum to Jerusalem. It's a song that is consistent with the love of a Creator who entered our world and, through the scars of death, proved the worth of every person and provided the means to draw out the best in them.

For Discussion:

1. What was your reaction to Princess Diana's death? to Mother Teresa's?

2. Who believed in you when you didn't believe in yourself?

3. Does Jesus' comfort level with unbelievers challenge you in any way? If so, how?

4. Describe those who live around you. What are some of their needs?

5. What are some ways you can find to draw out the best in these people? What steps are you willing to take to begin doing so?

The Proof

*If you know who you are
and to whom you belong
you don't have to
prove that you're right.
But to prove that you care
may require a towel
and a basin
of warm, soapy suds.*

—gea

CHAPTER FOUR

Aiming the Spotlight at Others

Jack Martens is a unique man. For one thing, he stands out in a crowd. This 6' 2", 230-pound middle school teacher has a bald head, a shaggy red and gray beard, and a mad cackle of a laugh. For another, he stands head and shoulders above many others in his profession. Since 1968, Jack has taught music to seventh and eighth graders at Benjamin Frankin Middle School in the inner city of San Francisco. Most of his students come from broken homes where welfare checks buy booze and dope. Music education was hardly a value. "Seeing those empty eyes longing for affection got my focus off myself," Jack admits.

Despite the odds, Jack thought music just might be the non-threatening means to reach his students. If he could get them to believe in their ability to play an instrument, they might be able to leave the psychological ghettoes that held them hostage. To that end, Jack put in 10 to 12 hours a day teaching himself to play every instrument the school owned. He knew the violin, piano, and a little trumpet, but not much beyond that. If he could learn to play, so could they. And learn they did. The small, struggling, music program at Franklin Middle School blossomed.

But the kids know he is not just at the school to teach them how to play an instrument. Even at their tender age, they understand his mission is to teach them life values—social skills, self-worth, self-discipline, and cooperation—through music. When they face a crisis, they ask him what he thinks. Jack Martens is a teacher who believes in being a servant to his students. He lets the kids eat lunch with him in his office. He helps them with difficult music passages before school. He has even braved riding in an elevator soiled with human feces on his way to deliver an instrument to one of his students who lived in a tenement apartment.

As a Christian, Jack is only too willing to share how his faith has sustained him. He keeps a Bible on his desk as a silent witness.

Because of his determination and faithful service, Jack Martens is one of the most celebrated educators in the State of California. He is well aware of his ability and experience. He knows he could teach wherever he applied. Still, after 32 years, he has chosen to remain at one of the most challenging schools anywhere. Enrollment has decreased by a third, and district funding for music has all but evaporated. Eighty percent of the kids' parents are on public assistance, and sixty percent of the parents do not speak English fluently. Seventy-five percent of the students are academically behind the grade level for their age.

So why does Jack stay at Benjamin Franklin Middle School? In his own words, he explains, "This corner of God's multiethnic kingdom is a glorious mission field. I have the privilege of taking up the basin and towel, just like Jesus did!"

I know Jack Martens personally. For several years he channeled his servant instincts as a volunteer musician in the church I pastored in northern California. If I didn't know better, I would have thought the delightful movie, *Mr. Holland's Opus,* was based on Jack's life. From Jack, I have learned more than a few grace notes about the rewards that come from a life of service. But nowhere is the example of self-denial more inspiring than in the One after whom my friend models his life.

Jesus knew his identity yet served with humility. Picture him on the banks of the muddy Jordan River. It's not the pristine sparkling water you might imagine. I've been there. Jesus was there. So were scores of others on the day I have in mind.

Jesus knew his identity yet served with humility.

John the Baptist was waist deep in the river, inviting repentant sinners, one at a time, to join him in the water. Are you picturing this? It was a hodge-podge congregation down by the riverside: drunks, prostitutes, adulterers, Pharisees, some who couldn't see, some with law degrees, some with no pedigree or respectability.

And who was in the midst of the crowd, waiting his turn in the water? You guessed it. Jesus was standing in line, linked with the chattel of first-century Israel.

He knew who he was, the unstained Son of God. Here was the only morally innocent man ever confined to the creature's finite cage. No symbolic water needed to cleanse his perfect heart. But he waited his turn in line nonetheless.

Once he stepped into the dirty water, the Baptist recognized him. Of course he would have.

Their mothers were cousins. They had probably played together as boys. They'd grown up with regular contact, perhaps comparing their individual senses of destiny. John knew the secret others were yet to be let in on. His mother's cousin's firstborn was God's promised Messiah.

So when Jesus met him midway in the Jordan, the Baptist spoke out: "What gives, Jesus? You don't need to be baptized by me. If anything, I need to be baptized by you! I'm not worthy to even unlatch your leather thongs" (Matthew 3:14, paraphrased).

But Jesus insisted. He knew he didn't need to be baptized, but—ironically—that is why he wanted to be. When humility is the cadence of your heart, you're not worried that the water is muddy or your reputation might be hurt when you're seen in a crowd with low-lifers. When the melody of your life is a series of grace notes, you don't let the title on your business card keep you from tooting another's horn.

In Philippians 2, the apostle Paul describes Jesus' incarnation in a similar way. He willingly removed his kingly robes and came to earth, taking on the role of a servant. In the process, he identified with the needs of those he came to serve. Here is someone who completely understands our situation and is in a unique role to intercede in our behalf.

Knowing Your Identity

In our Lord's actions the night before he died, we see yet another example of his propensity for humility. It was a familiar upper room. Jesus and his associates had gathered there before. But on this night, a heavy cloud draped that familiar room with a scratchy fabric of uncertainty.

Between courses of the traditional supper, Jesus acted in a very unfamiliar manner. He got up from the table, left the room, and returned with a basin of water and a towel. Removing his outer robe, Jesus proceeded to circle the table and wash the feet of the disciples. I say unfamiliar because foot washing was the task assigned to a common servant or slave. While washing feet was a necessity of the culture—given the amount of foot traffic, sandaled feet, and unpaved streets—it was unheard of for a teacher to wash the feet of his students.

According to the apostle John's account, Peter was the only one who objected to Jesus' demeaning role. The fisherman-turned-disciple reacted quite strongly. But, as was often the case, Jesus challenged Peter's pontificating and kept right on scrubbing filthy feet.

And as he washed and dried callused toes and heels, kneeling all the while in a posture of humility, Jesus explained his actions. He was giving them an example of how they should behave. In essence, he said, "Even if teachers normally don't wash feet, I refuse to place myself on a pedestal of pride. I've denied my privileges in order to be a servant. And I expect the same of you" (John 13:13–15, paraphrased).

The first college-level Bible course I ever took was as a freshman at Seattle Pacific University. The class was simply called "Gospel of Mark." My professor was a short, bearded man in his fifties. His eyes flamed with intensity and passion. His breath betrayed his love of garlic. His teaching style was dramatic and engaging. I loved to sit in his class (as long as I was sitting at least 10 feet away) and take notes. I'm sure I must have learned a great deal about the literary style Mark used or the cultural context in which he wrote. But the only thing I recall about Dr. Davis's countless lectures was a statement he made over and over again. "Class, always remember the key verse of the entire Gospel. It's Mark 10:45, where Jesus candidly confesses his reason for coming to earth: 'For even the Son of Man did not come to be served, but to serve, and to give his life as a ransom for many.'"

Why was it the key verse of Mark's gospel? Dr. Davis was quick to conjecture. For one thing, Mark focused all his energy illustrating that verse in the teachings, miracles, and episodes of Jesus' life that he chose to include in his 16 chapters. For another, Jesus' disclosure of a servant-oriented life is so unexpected from One who had a divine right to demand homage and obedience from those whom he had created.

Well, 30 years later, I still remember what Dr. Davis said. And from what I've studied since, I would say that not only is Mark 10:45 the key verse in the Gospel of Mark, it is the key verse of Jesus' life. It is what motivated his decision to descend to earth.

Here's the way Eugene Peterson paraphrases the first several verses of Philippians 2:

> Don't push your way to the front; don't sweet-talk your way to the top. Put yourself aside, and help others get ahead. Don't be obsessed with getting your own advantage. Forget yourself long enough to lend a helping hand.
>
> Think of yourselves the way Christ Jesus thought of himself. He had equal status with God but didn't think so much of himself that he had to cling to the

advantages of that status no matter what. Not at all. When the time came, he set aside the privileges of deity and took on the status of a slave, became *human!* Having become human, he stayed human. It was an incredibly humbling process. He didn't claim special privileges. Instead, he lived a selfless, obedient life and then died a selfless, obedient death. (*The Message,* Philippians 2:3–8)

I love the freshness of Peterson's translation. Jesus is not "God in a costume." He really did lay aside his divine prerogatives to embrace life as we know it at this end of Eden and on this side of heaven.

Jesus is not "God in a costume." He really did lay aside his divine prerogatives to embrace life as we know it.

By his own choice, he became incarcerated in the creature's cage, imprisoned by human skin, desires, needs, and pain. Jesus knew his true identity but refused to let his title take precedence over our plight as sinners in need of a Savior.

Toward the beginning of King Hussein of Jordan's reign, late one night, disguised in street clothes, the king secretly left the palace. With the help of a friend, he borrowed a taxi and pretended to be a cab driver. In the wee hours of the morning, King Hussein drove through the streets of Amman and picked up fares. As his passengers sat in the back seat, unaware of the true identity of their driver, he asked about their hopes and concerns. He even asked what they thought of the new king who had come into power. Now, there's a servant-hearted approach to leadership!

We may never fully understand the sensation of the Incarnation until we accept the fact that Jesus was one with us in every regard except sin. Those who rubbed shoulders with Jesus day after day saw a person who got dog tired, loved to eat, enjoyed a glass of wine, struggled with lustful thoughts, felt physical pain when he pulled a muscle and emotional pain when he felt deserted. Jesus even knew what it was like to question the Father's will and feel alienated from him.

Jesus laid aside his only begotten bigshot-ness to accomplish what we most needed and to give us an example at the same time. Notice, I said he laid down his divine prerogatives, not relinquished them. Jesus knew his identity, yet he chose to serve with humility. That is exactly what the gospel writer says as he introduces Jesus' actions in the upper room. "Jesus knew that the Father had put all things under his power, and that he had come from God and was returning to God; so he got up from the meal, took off his outer clothing, and wrapped a towel around his waist" (John 13:3–4).

It doesn't take a band director's ear to hear the drumbeat of love that pulsates in those two verses. Jesus marched to a cadence most people couldn't hear. He knew who he was. He knew who called him Son. He knew his cosmic title: "God exalted him to the highest place and gave him a name that is above every name, that at the name of Jesus every knee should bow . . . and every tongue confess that Jesus Christ is Lord, to the glory of God the Father" (Philippians 2:9–11). And because he did, he didn't need it engraved on a brass name plate. When you know your true status, it doesn't matter all that much if nobody else recognizes you.

The same concept is developed in Hebrews 12:2. I wonder whether you've ever read that great wall-plaque verse with a sense of Jesus' self-awareness? It's a telling commentary that explains his willingness and determination to keep the servant's towel cinched around his waist.

Through the example of Jesus, the writer of Hebrews attempts to motivate Christians who have grown tired of denying themselves: "Let us fix our eyes on Jesus, the author and perfecter of our faith, who for the joy set before him endured the cross, scorning its shame, and sat down at the right hand of the throne of God." Because Jesus knew his birthright and inheritance, he kept the needle of his compass pointed toward fulfilling the needs of those who needed him.

Richard McDonald and his brother Maurice started a drive-in restaurant in San Bernardino, California, in the late '40s. It featured 15-cent hamburgers, 19-cent cheeseburgers, 20-cent milkshakes, and 10-cent fries. Within a few years, business mogul Ray Kroc bought the proprietary rights, and the McDonald's fast-food industry was born.

When Richard McDonald died in the summer of 1998 at the age of 89, it was revealed that the namesake of the most famous fast-food chain in history frequently ate at the McDonald's near his home. He always ordered a cheeseburger, a shake, and fries. But, much to the chagrin of his grandchildren, he never identified himself to the employees, never cut in line, and always paid full price.

Self-denial may be termed inappropriate by those who trade in titles and protocol, but it is the currency of those who would spend their lives emulating Jesus. John prefaces his account of the foot-washing episode by saying that Jesus used this object lesson as a vehicle to communicate the full extent of his love. In other words, being a servant, not just acting like one, is the ultimate way to prove your concern and commitment to another.

Dare to Care

In the summer of 1995, a junior from Wheaton College claimed the crown of Miss Illinois. Tracy Hayes was quite outspoken about her desire to be Miss America. Her blue eyes sparkled with excitement as she described the rewards and opportunities that envied title would provide. But Tracy was equally as outspoken about her person relationship with Jesus Christ. She has committed her life and her future to him. Whether or not she would be the judges' choice in Atlantic City, she knew The People's Choice would choreograph her circumstances according to his will for her life.

Because we live near Wheaton College, my family felt a bond with Tracy. We hoped she'd win on the night of the Miss America pageant. We sat in front of our TV, cheering for Miss Illinois. We were disappointed when Tracy was not selected, but our disappointment was dwarfed a few weeks later when Tracy accepted my invitation to give her testimony at our church and then have dinner with our family.

As we sat around the dinner table, it warmed my heart to see my three beautiful daughters relate comfortably to someone they considered a celebrity. But as Tracy shared, we all were impressed with the way she placed physical beauty and fame in perspective. For her, serving Jesus and caring for hurting people were far more important than parading on a stage in an evening gown or accepting the praise of fickle fans who envy the crown you wear.

Tracy described her volunteer work with juvenile delinquents as the highest joy in her young life. Even though she was attractive, smart, popular, and Miss Illinois, her purpose on planet Earth was grounded in others, not herself. I have no doubt Tracy's winsome witness rubbed off on the three Miss Americas who call me Dad.

If we know who we are in Christ, that leaves us with a demanding task: putting aside our culture's conditioning that would lead us to esteem title and prestige as the goals of our lives.

Recently, as part of her responsibilities as a member of the junior-high missions team, my middle daughter invited me to work with her at a homeless shelter. Having never done anything like that before, I didn't quite know what to expect.

We arranged mattresses on the floor, making up each mattress with freshly laundered linen. I tried to imagine who would be sleeping on the beds I was making. Would they be young? Would an old man be able to stoop to sleep on a four-inch-thick mattress resting on a hardwood floor? Would there be children? I was overwhelmed with gratitude for the king-size bed I sleep in, cuddled next to a wife who adores me. It's a bed, I must admit, I take for granted.

Then we found our places behind the serving tables laden with hot, home-cooked food donated by people in our church. We filled out name tags and stuck them to our aprons. I suppose I could have written Rev. Asimakoupoulos or Pastor Greg. I didn't. On a lark, I simply printed "Oz"—a nickname I'd gone by in high school and college but hadn't used in more than 25 years.

As the doors were unlocked and our guests arrived, they came to our table. I dished out mashed potatoes and steamed broccoli. Curiously, most looked down and would not make eye contact unless addressed.

"Mashed potatoes? They're really good!"

A look up. A smile. "Yes, please!"

Several noticed my name tag. "That's your name? Oz?" One even asked if I was "The Wizard."

A wizard I'm not. But I am a son of God, a child of the King. I am a disciple of One who had it all and gave it all up in order to prove his love for a lost planet spinning out of control. I don't need to boast my title. I know who I am. And because I do, I am content to spell my name with acts of service.

I don't need to boast my title. I know who I am. And because I do, I am content to spell my name with acts of service.

Action Step 4 for the 50-Day Spiritual Adventure is called "Dare to Care." It provides us an opportunity to deny our self-centered instincts and demonstrate a sensitivity to others. Such a demonstration is not natural. It calls for swimming upstream against the current of convenience and personal agendas. It is not easy, nor is it always desirable. You see why it's called *Dare* to Care?

Even Jesus, though sinless, was tempted by pride, ambition, and selfishness. He was a son of Adam as well as the Son of God. But he pushed hard against the gravitational pull of a fallen planet. He knew his identity, but he also knew his vulnerability. Such knowledge led him to rely on the Holy Spirit as he denied himself. And that denial of himself is what we see in his symbolic act of washing his disciples' feet.

Literal foot-washing would be a little weird these days, but what other kinds of things could we do?

★ Mow a neighbor's lawn
★ Help a coworker with a project
★ Pay school tuition for a kid in a struggling family
★ Offer free babysitting for a single mom
★ Visit the residents of a nursing home—and maybe even wash their feet

Once a week, do an act of service for someone who's not a Christian. (You don't need to grill them about their religious beliefs, just don't target those you already know are believers. This action step is about reaching out to those who still need to meet Jesus.) Be sure to serve with a humble, Christlike attitude—not grudgingly. Tune in to other people's needs, not just your own need to meet needs. It's about them, not you.

Obviously, it is ultimately about Jesus, but be patient about this. Perhaps your service will also give you a chance to talk about your faith, but don't be primarily concerned about that up front. If someone thinks you're serving just to fill a "kingdom quota," it won't mean much. Offer genuine service from the heart of love that Jesus gives you. Then, if the opportunity arises, let them know that Jesus is the One they should thank.

Daring to care is an overlooked ingredient in a recipe for "celebration stew." More and more people will taste the goodness of the Lord and give their lives over to him when we surprise them with simple, unexpected acts of love. The old saw is true: People don't care how much we know until they know how much we care.

Sometimes daring to care means you take a chance and live on the edge a little. It might require swallowing your pride and not being concerned what others think. That has freed me up to be more innovative in my preaching and in the way I respond to the requests of those God is drawing to himself.

After pastoring a church in California for 11 years, the time came to say goodbye. Wendy and I were showered with all kinds of wonderful gifts: a painting by Thomas Kinkaide, beautiful wall hangings, a crystal vase, and a French Psalter from the 1600s to add to my prized collection of hymnbooks.

But the most meaningful gift of all arrived just a few days before I moved. It was camouflaged as an invitation to play golf with my friend Marty Koll. That was a round of golf I'll never forget.

I remember when Marty first visited our church seven years earlier. After much family coercion, he reluctantly agreed to accompany his wife and two daughters. Marty had been turned off by institutional religion long before. As far as he was concerned, Sunday mornings were best spent on the golf course.

I met the Koll family in the parking lot after worship had begun. They arrived late, and there I was hiding out among the cars in a Middle-eastern robe. I didn't want to spoil the effect of my first-person illustrated sermon by being seen by the congregation beforehand. I could read Marty's face. After seeing me, he was less sure than ever about giving church another chance. Was that the *pastor* without shoes and in a bathrobe? What kind of church was this?

Fortunately, the worship folder that morning promoted the annual men's golf tournament the following Saturday. Barefoot sermons aside, golf was a language Marty spoke. He signed up for the golf outing, and when the tournament arrived, so did Marty, with a sparkle in his eye. I had no idea he was a ringer. Needless to say, he won.

The organizer of the tournament asked Marty if he could be in church the next day. It was customary to present the trophy in front of the congregation. Marty complied. Whether it was the fact that I wore a coat and tie and shoes that Sunday, or that the young adult class warmly received Marty and his wife, I'll never know. What matters is what resulted. They decided to continue attending our church.

Within a few months, Marty's two elementary-aged daughters prayed with their Sunday school teachers to receive Jesus as Savior. Shortly thereafter, Kristy and Jenny began to ask their parents questions about their new faith. Marty and Cindy quickly realized they needed to make the same commitment as their daughters.

At the end of one sermon I looked out over the congregation as we prayed. I asked those who were willing to entrust their lives to the Lord to lift their heads and look me in the eye. Marty and Cindy returned my gaze. Because Marty's dad had died in a car accident before he was even born, Marty responded with childlike enthusiasm as I introduced him to the fatherlike love of God in the week that followed.

Within a matter of a few months, his tender faith was tested. He watched his mother wither from cancer and die. About that same time, I was wrestling with my father's near-fatal heart attack. We found consolation following little white balls around the golf course and praying for each other. Our friendship grew.

> **We found consolation following little white balls around the golf course and praying for each other.**

The Koll family entered fully into the life of our church and community. Cindy was elected president of the local PTA, Marty became our church custodian. Together, they gave leadership to the Sunday school class that initially welcomed them with friendship. For me, one of the personal joys of the Christmas season was watching Marty play Santa Claus following our annual carol sing at the convalescent hospital.

For some reason known only to Marty, he was never baptized as a testimony to his new birth. Still, we found ourselves sharing our love for the Lord and sharing time on the golf course where we unintentionally "baptized" many a golf ball. The years sped by.

And then came the invitation to play golf one last time before I moved. The day seemed perfect. The weather was ideal and my game was on. In addition, Marty and I were joined by two of our best friends from church. There was laughter and honest conversation about meaningful issues. I swallowed hard, realizing I'd soon be 2,000 miles removed from these men I'd grown to love as brothers.

As we approached the gorgeous ninth tee, complete with a meandering brook and a cascading waterfall, Marty surprised me with a question. "Pastor Greg, would you baptize me?" I shrugged off his query, thinking he was joking, and reached for my driver. Marty reached in his golf bag and retrieved the Bible I'd given him the day he became a Christian. "I'm serious," he said, handing me the Bible. "You know I've never been baptized. And . . . well . . . here's water. What's standing in the way?"

My open mouth widened into a smile as my eyes teared up. I had a choice. I could insist on the baptism protocol I'd learned in my seminary training and encourage Marty to have the new pastor seal his commitment in a subsequent worship service after I'd moved. Or, I could live on the edge and not be concerned about what my seminary professors—or the threesome on the tee behind us watching our every move—would think. I had a pretty good idea what Jesus would have done. And then I remembered the Ethiopian's request of Philip in Acts 8 and decided there was a precedent for unorthodox baptisms.

Removing our shoes and socks and rolling up our slacks, Marty and I stepped into the flowing brook. While our friends looked on, I read aloud Psalm 23. Somehow "green pastures" and "still waters" seemed appropriate. I quizzed Marty about his faith in Christ and applauded his boldness. Asking God to transform the gurgling stream into a means of grace, I baptized Marty in the name of the Father, Son, and Holy Spirit.

At that moment a reservoir of memories flooded my mind. I thought of all the "Martys" God had allowed me to touch in 11 brief years and the "Martys" I'd not yet met at my new church. My heart throbbed with joy and gratitude. I welcomed my brother with a bear hug as he stepped out of the water.

A circle of four men held hands and prayed God's blessing on Marty as the threesome behind us watched. They smiled their approval, although I'm not exactly sure what they thought was going on. What a sight it must have been. For a moment in time, a water hazard on the ninth hole became holy ground, where the love of God converged with love of golf. In spite of my identity as a revered clergyman in the community, I left my preaching robe in the closet and wrapped a towel around my waist instead.

A Servant to the End

I'm learning how to take my cues from One who, when faced with the choice of accepting honor or giving in to humility, never batted an eye but focused on serving others. Even on the cross, when Jesus was hanging naked, a servant's towel could be seen tied around his waist. In unimagined anguish, bleeding profusely and writhing in pain, Jesus hung in there for you and me.

As the old gospel song puts it, "He could have called ten thousand angels to destroy the world and set him free. He could have called ten thousand angels, but he died alone for you and me." The holy King of Glory did not deserve to be treated as a common criminal, but he voluntarily laid aside his title in order to entitle us to eternal life. The One we see nailed to a cross is humility incarnate. He was a servant in life. He could be nothing else in death.

As Jesus struggled to breathe, he had no choice but to put his weight on his spiked feet and slide up the splintered vertical shaft in an effort to leverage his lungs. He was in agony, but not only physical agony. His spirit panted under the collective sin of all humanity. The demons

danced on his dying soul. And yet in the midst
of his horrific death, Jesus saw his weeping mother sobbing at his feet. The pounding heart of
heaven's Prince broke for Mary. He was moved
with compassion for her. With what little
strength he had left, in humility, he served her
needs. Straining to speak, he called John to care
for his mother. A servant to the end.

In something of an irony, The People's Choice
found his earthly identity in choosing people
instead of himself. He taught his disciples that the
greatest expression of love was to be willing to lay
down one's life for one's friends. Jesus practiced
what he preached. But in his practice, he raised
the bar. He not only lay down his life for those
who viewed themselves as his friends, he died for
those who unabashedly took pride in the fact that
they were his enemies. In this man, we see a historical figure that others have repeatedly tried to
emulate in parable, fiction, and film.

As a rule, I don't like swashbuckling action
flicks. Unlike most of my friends, I haven't seen
the *Indiana Jones* movies or the endless series of
Star Trek releases. So when my wife, who does
enjoy high adventure, said she wanted to see *The
Mask of Zorro*, I swallowed hard to keep my gut
reaction in my gut. I had to remember that
Wendy, having grown up on the mission field in
Mexico, had seen the original *Zorro* movies in
black and white as a child. For her, the thought of
seeing the new Zorro was a way of celebrating her
first-hand appreciation of the Mexican frontier.

Determined to put my own interests aside, I
seized upon what I saw as an opportunity to serve
my sweetheart. It was a night to remember. Dinner
at a favorite Mexican restaurant and then the theater. I even sprang for popcorn and a large soda.

Well, I have to admit Anthony Hopkins and Antonio Banderas challenged my *carte blanche* prejudice of high drama. *The Mask of Zorro* was a decent film. And yes, I even walked away with a spiritual application.

If you've seen the film, you know that the plot begins by showing the heartless cruelty of the Spanish governor who, with a company of wealthy landowners, serves Spain's interests in California. The peasants have obviously been mistreated by those who flaunt their wealth and power. A handful of rebels who dared to fight for freedom and justice are about to be executed. But just in time, the legendary masked savior surfaces and frees the condemned.

Just in time, the legendary masked savior surfaces and frees the condemned.

Within the first quarter hour of the movie, we discover the identity of Zorro. He is one of the wealthy landowners who covers his powerful profile in order to serve the needs of the commoners. Secure in his position, flanked by substantial finances, Don Diego de la Vega withstands the criticism of those who say he is a traitor to his country and his class. His redemptive missions reveal his heart, even as he conceals his true identity. Donning his black blouse, black trousers, black boots, black hat, and signature black mask, he rides his black horse, Tornado, from his grandiose estate to the lean-tos of meager villages, where some poor soul needs saving.

Can you believe it? A film I didn't want to see, I can't get out of my head. It gripped my heart. In the character of Zorro, I see a picture of my Savior's love for me. No, Christ didn't wear a mask, but he *did* mask his glory in an effort to draw near to people. Jesus did not wield a saber by which he left his mark on walls or tapestries or doors. His calling card was a basin and towel. He left it in that familiar upper room, but not just there. He left it everywhere he went. "The Son of Man did not come to be served, but to serve, and to give his life as a ransom for many" (Mark 10:45).

Thinking about Wendy's love of adventure movies gives me pause to celebrate her unique talents. Wendy is a gifted teacher, linguist, and home economist. Her skills with Spanish and French, education, and culinary arts have been attested to by students, parishioners, and neighbors.

What is just as impressive to me is Wendy's willingness to deny herself the recognition and monetary rewards that come with a job outside our home in order serve the needs of our three school-aged daughters. She is well aware of her competencies, yet, like her Savior, finds deep fulfillment in giving her life away.

Adoniram Judson had a wife like that. While still a bachelor, the first American missionary was attracted to Nancy Hazeltine's self-awareness and God-consciousness. All he longed for in a life companion was encapsulated in this wealthy aristocrat's daughter.

Judson, seeking permission to marry Nancy, asked her father if he was prepared to never see his daughter again because of the risks associated with world evangelization in the eighteenth century. Mr. Hazeltine recognized the weightiness of the young missionary's request but said the decision was up to his daughter.

One biographer records Nancy's response this way:

I have made my decision to walk away
from all the comforts of family and
friends to go to a land I have never been
to and from where I may never return . . .
to die there alone maybe and lose all. I
have made my decision. As God is my
witness I will not decline the offer and
privilege to give my life to rescue the perishing. (*Seek Only God's Approval:* A
Message by K. P. Yohannan, Gospel for
Asia, Carrolton, Tex.)

Nancy Hazeltine Judson never did see her father
again. She died on the mission field, a young
wife and mother with no regrets. She was convinced that she had made the right choice. Scores
of converts found their Savior because she had
been willing to serve with humility.

Are you willing to do the same? Can you
make an effort to turn the spotlight from yourself
and aim it toward others who need love and
care? Then you must ask yourself, who might
those people be? For Nancy Judson, they were
pagans in a land far away. For Jack Martens, they
were kids in the inner city. For Zorro, they were
unfortunate neighbors in his own town.

And for Jesus, they were the entire world.
"The Son of Man came not to be served, but to
serve, and to give his life as a ransom for many."

For Discussion:

1. What teacher did you have in school who had
a profound influence on your values and career
choice?

2. Would Mark 10:45 describe your mission in life? Why or why not?

3. What examples of Jesus' humility inspire you? Which ones do you struggle with?

4. Other than *Mr. Holland's Opus* or *The Mask of Zorro,* what movies, plays, or television shows have you seen that offer examples of Jesus' determination to give his life away in acts of humble service?

5. What steps are you willing to take to dare to care for others as Jesus did?

A Master Artist

He spoke a dialect
he knew would connect
with the poor and rich,
commoners, kings.
On the canvas
of curious minds,
he painted with words.
Parables and stories,
metaphoric grace.
He created masterpieces
using what was commonplace.

—gea

CHAPTER
FIVE

A Script with the Audience in Mind

LEARNING THE LANGUAGE of a new congregation can be a real challenge. Wanna see my battle scars? When I graduated from seminary I left with more than a ministerial license and a trunk full of books. I moved to my first church with what I believed to be an enlightened understanding of what worship was to look like, sound like, and—at times—even smell like. After all, I had studied the evolution of liturgy from the Old Testament through the Protestant Reformation and had reveled in the development of what, to me, was elaborate, beautiful, and meaningful.

I loved the great hymns of the faith. Growing up in a small Pentecostal church, I was weaned on gospel songs and worship choruses. But it wasn't until I went away to a Christian college that I discovered the rich hymnody of the church and the glorious sound of a pipe organ. Daily chapel services at Seattle Pacific University were a pivotal part of my spiritual formation. I came to appreciate the Apostles' Creed and the Doxology as communal links with the saints of another age. Confession of sin, assurance of pardon, the Lord's Prayer, and various responses came to be desired components in my definition of corporate worship. Banners, symbols, and ceremony had become the ecstatic utterance of my artistically sensitive spirit.

Shortly after unpacking my books, reality set in. The people, lovable as they were, nonetheless seemed ignorant of what "true worship" was and how it "should" be practiced—at least according to what I'd learned in seminary. Frankly, I was embarrassed by the casual, unsophisticated, freestyle flow of Sunday morning worship with my first congregation. Their hymnody consisted of off-the-wall choruses projected overhead. Their disorder of worship included prayer-and-share time every Sunday, which I felt smacked of the "superficial" testimony services I remembered from childhood. (It also tended to cut into my sermon time.) What's more, the church had a habit of singing "We Are One in the Bond of Love" as the benediction. *How pedestrian!* I thought.

I determined to waste no time attempting to raise their level of understanding. I insisted on congregational responses, unison readings, corporate prayers of confession, periods of silence, and meaty hymns. I gave the sign of the cross as part of the benediction and even took to wearing a cross medallion as a symbol of my call.

Looking back to that situation almost 20 years ago, I'm ashamed of how arrogant I was. As I introduced a more liturgical structure—one that may have made my professors proud—I should have also taken to wearing a collar. Not a clerical collar, but the kind you get from a pharmacy for a stiff neck.

It's true, as a pastor and teacher I had much to impart about worship. I sincerely wanted to lead the people the Lord had called me to serve. But there was a language problem. I was insensitive to the congregation's traditions and needs

and oblivious to their culture. No wonder I felt
continually frustrated! I didn't understand their
dialect, and what I was speaking certainly was
"Greek" to them.

If those of us in the church don't always
speak the same dialect, you can be sure we typi-
cally do not communicate in the same language
as those outside the church. For example, what
would my next-door neighbor, Scott, who spends
his Sunday mornings manicuring his enviable
front yard, think if he was invited to one of our
churches and heard the pastor eloquently address
the congregation with the following exhortation?

"Praise the Lamb! Isn't it a blessing to know
that your transgressions have been nailed to the
Tree? If you've been justified by the atoning sac-
rifice of the Beloved, you've been sanctified by
the infilling of the Holy Ghost. Hallelujah, Bride!
We're marching to Zion, bringing in the sheaves,
and waiting for the Rapture. And all because
there is a fountain filled with blood drawn from
Immanuel's veins."

Wow! Can you imagine? If Scott ever did
returned to church, he'd probably ask me if I
owned a lexicon of Christianese he could borrow.
Now, granted, that was a bit of an exaggeration.
But when is the last time you have listened to the
coded expressions in the pulpit from the vantage
point of someone who doesn't know the code?

Preachers aren't the only ones who are guilty
of speaking a language many people can't understand. We who have been Christians for any
length of time usually begin to do the same.
Sadly, when those we are called to reach with the
Good News overhear our conversations, it's all
Greek to them, too.

A Master Communicator

Speaking of Greek: While visiting my grandfather's homeland a number of years ago, I
attempted to use what little modern Greek I
knew. I asked a shopkeeper how much a certain
article of clothing cost. Her guffaw was unexpected and embarrassing. Later, I learned the cause of
her uncontained laughter—I had unashamedly
inquired how much *I* cost! My attempt to add to
my wardrobe would have been simplified if I had
taken the time to really learn the language.

I did walk away with more than a souvenir. I
took to heart a principle that would serve me
well for years to come as a pastor. In order to
reach those you want to understand *you*, you
have to understand *their* perspective and communicate accordingly.

Jesus grasped that principle instinctively. He
was a master communicator. He didn't begin
with what he had to say; he began by crawling
inside the heart of his hearers so he knew what
images and symbols, expressions and values they
connected with. Based upon what he understood,
he clothed his words in fabric people could recognize. Call it *incarnational communication*. When
we use the word *incarnation*, we think of God
becoming a human being. And that's what incarnation means: "And the Word became flesh and
made his dwelling among us" (John 1:14). In
Jesus, God the Father "expressed" his holiness,
mercy, judgment, and love in a form we could
identify with. In order to fully relate to us and
experience our plight as human beings, Jesus had
to become one of us.

Yet the word *incarnation* is not limited to
God's physical visitation of earth. It also means
"to embody in flesh, to put an idea into concrete

form." Whereas God disclosed himself and his love in concrete form by sending Jesus, Jesus followed his Father's strategy of speaking in everyday language that ordinary people could understand. This can be clearly seen in the way he attracted people and in the message he shared with them: *A farmer went out to plant seed. . . . A man went on a journey. . . . A woman had ten silver coins and lost one. . . . There was a father who had two sons.*

The way Jesus communicated separated him from the other rabbis of his day. He was in a class by himself. "He doesn't lecture the way the teachers of the law teach!" the villagers of Capernaum observed. "He doesn't quote endless sources. He speaks authoritatively."

Well, admittedly, that's a paraphrase of what is recorded in Mark 1:22, but it captures the essence of what captured people. For one thing, Jesus didn't require an annotated bibliography of footnoted references. Unlike the others who taught in the local synagogues, he was an expert in his field. He just told it like it was. He didn't have to cite Rabbi Simon or Rabbi Tevya to bolster the strength of his claims. And that, in and of itself, was a break with tradition.

The Gospel of Mark implies something else about the people's reaction to Jesus' approach. Jesus was concerned with teaching people about the Scriptures, while the teachers of the law were committed to teaching the Scriptures. Can you tell the difference in these two approaches? One is people-centered, the other is content-centered.

Jesus' passion was people. He lived with people. He loved people. He cried with people. He challenged people who were addicted to self-destructive behavior. His aim was to communicate the values of the Creator to creatures who were incapable of seeing him. Jesus came to earth to translate the heartbeat of a loving God into a language common people could understand. And to that end, he played the part of a world-class linguist, observing the dialect of culture and lifestyle so his out-of-this-world message could be grasped and valued. Like a professor I had in seminary used to say, "The cookies were put on the bottom shelf so they could be easily reached."

Jesus spoke God's truth in everyday language.

One of Jesus' favorite expressions was this: *The kingdom of God is like. . . .* With those words, he introduced us to parables and proverbs, similes and stories that reduced the Torah to tablets small enough to chew and digest. He was the master of the metaphor. And because he hung out on street corners instead of on Mt. Sinai, he was able to speak God's truth in the language of the people

The kingdom of God is like a mustard seed. The kingdom of God is like yeast that a woman took and mixed in a large amount of flour. The kingdom of God is like hidden treasure in a field. The kingdom of God is like a net that was let down into the lake. When the disciples heard Jesus begin a story with those words, they became like little children, eager to listen.

Do you remember when your parents or grandparents would tuck you in at night with a story that began "Once upon a time . . . ," and your body relaxed as that familiar voice unlocked your imagination and opened the door of your mind to the lessons of life? Those fairytales or fables were not just sleep enhancers. They were couriers of truth. *Little Red Riding Hood* taught us not to go into the woods alone. From *The Boy Who Cried Wolf,* we learned the consequences of lying. In *Cinderella,* we discovered how to hope for justice while maintaining a servant heart.

In recent years, many seminaries have altered the way they teach preaching. For decades, the standard fare was expository preaching. A preacher walked through a passage of Scripture, hanging theological points and suggested applications on an outline of thought to which the verses in question lent themselves. Sometimes, to assist the congregation in remembering the three points of the outline, the first word of each point would begin with the same letter.

But research into the way people learn has changed this traditional approach to homiletics. The lecture format is the least effective style of learning. Communication techniques that allow the listener to interact with the message through imagination and the senses is much more memorable and motivating.

Radio broadcaster Paul Harvey believes in the persuasive power of art. He is one of my favorite commentators on culture. He has a way of turning truth on its head in order to help us see in new ways. I recently came across this statement from Paul Harvey entitled *The Power of Art over Argument.*

The power of art over argument. Nobody could have persuaded a generation to produce a baby boom—yet Shirley Temple movies made every couple want to have one. Military enlistments were lagging for our Air Force until, almost overnight, a movie called *Top Gun* had recruits standing in line. The power of art over argument. . . . British sweatshops for children existed only until Dickens wrote about them. American slaves were slaves only until Harriet Beecher Stowe wrote about them. Oh, yes, Lincoln himself credited her with having started the Civil War. The power of art over argument. . . . You want to convince the unconvinced? Don't call to arms—call to art! *(As quoted by Kurt Brunner of Focus on the Family in a talk given April 15, 1999.)*

Pablo Picasso, a controversial artist of the last century, echoes Paul Harvey's sentiments. Picasso celebrated the mystery of art this way: "Art is a lie that tells the truth!" You may have to read it over a couple of times to catch his drift. What he meant is that though a piece of art may not be "true" in the sense of factual or realistic, it carries a truth we understand by intuition. I believe that is why Jesus liked to tell stories. It's one of the reasons he attracted such a wide audience. In painting, poetry, or parables—as well as in novels, plays, or TV shows—the essence of God's truth comes through, even though the scripts or images have been made up. All stories are a shadowy reflection of *his*-story.

Amazing, isn't it? Showing rather than telling is a more effective way of communicating with people. A story does just that. As a result, more and more professors of preaching are advocating narrative preaching: scripting a sermon much like a screenwriter would write a plot for a movie, retelling the stories in the Bible in a way that enables people in the pews to put themselves into the biblical episode.

Narrative preaching still places a priority on identifying the authoritative truth of God's Word, but it alters the way the truth is delivered. And part of the effective delivery system is finding the images and metaphors that are current with the culture and life experience of the listeners. How curious that we are finally getting back to the way Jesus engaged his audiences!

A Natural Bridge

In the early '70s, a motion picture came out of Hollywood that troubled some Christians. Others thought it was terrific. *Godspell* was one of the first cinematic attempts to adapt the life and message of Jesus for the contemporary culture. Watching it nearly 30 years after it was released, you can see how much it was stylized to fit the post-hippie era of psychedelic expressions of peace, love, and free speech. But that was intentional. The producers of *Godspell* aimed their script at an audience who'd learned their version of English at the feet of James Taylor, not King James. That's why the tag line for the 1973 offering was "The Gospel According to Today."

Long before Stephen Schwartz would wow theatergoers with his singable songs for *Pocahontas* and *The Prince of Egypt,* he wrote the lyrical score for *Godspell.* Even if you never saw the musical, you may have heard this song:

Day by day, day by day.
O, dear Lord, three things I pray.
To see you more clearly,
love you more dearly,
follow you more nearly
day by day.

Following the flow of Matthew's Gospel, David Greene and John Michael Tebelak collaborated on a screenplay that casts Jesus as a clownish leader of a traveling acting troupe. He attracts a most unlikely menagerie of characters to join his extended tour of New York City.

Seeing the Son of God painted as a clown bothered many. I chose to see it as a subtle way the world in which we live, and into which Jesus himself entered, is like a circus. The music of the musical is compelling. The story line is strangely accurate for a film that was not written or financed by evangelical believers. Because of that, I was more forgiving than some when the Resurrection scene was not overtly orthodox. Compared to the movie version of Broadway's *Jesus Christ Superstar,* released the same year, *Godspell* was tame—and more true to the Bible.

As far as I'm concerned, the pluses of this film far outweigh the minuses. Even though I don't have any flared bellbottom jeans or tie-dye shirts in my closet anymore, *Godspell* crosses the border into the land in which I live more easily than many religious films that attempt to recreate the culture of Palestine. The parables of Jesus come alive. His sense of humor is celebrated. The context of an urban city effectively translates the message of the kingdom into the world where most of us live.

> Movies and videos, television and plays, books and music can help us think "incarnationally."

For me, *Godspell* illustrates Jesus' style of incarnational communication. It helps me, as a Christian communicator, to put my message in a context that will enhance my effectiveness.

But a piece doesn't have to be about Jesus in order to help us understand his method of reaching the lost. Movies and videos, television and plays, books and music can help us think "incarnationally."

I have a friend who teaches contextual theology at Fuller Seminary in Southern California. In pursuit of his goal to train future pastors to effectively communicate the gospel, Rob's intellectual diet includes novels and movies. He believes it's time the church waves the white flag and passes the popcorn. According to Rob, "Far too often Hollywood and the church have regarded each other with distance, if not disdain. In reality, they have more in common than they would care to admit."

Granted, some films or shows are more inspirational than others. Take the long-running TV sitcom, *Home Improvement.* I liked it even before learning that one of the producers of the show taught drama at a Christian college in Illinois. For several years, our family faithfully followed the Taylors as they dealt with the same prickly issues all families face at some point: moral temptation, peer pressure, the death of a parent, friendships gone sour, job stress, health crises, marital staleness.

Tim and Jill Taylor certainly weren't saints, but they did show thoughtful judgment and made moral choices. Even the "face on the other side of the fence" was a symbol of sacred conscience. Wilson, the Taylors' backyard neighbor, was a wellspring of wisdom. His insights celebrated the value of friendship and the need for truth beyond ourselves. In *Home Improvement,* Hollywood took a well deserved bow. Not only did it improve the homes (and families) of those who watched it, it improved primetime television as well.

As part of the 50-Day Spiritual Adventure, you'll be given an opportunity to view the media in a new light. Many believe that movies and videos, as well as television, music, and other media outlets, are the most natural bridge to our non-Christian neighbors. They see these as the language most easily understood in North American culture. The majority of Christians and non-Christians go to the movies or watch TV. Whereas the front page or the sports page may have been the common denominator at the water cooler 10 years ago, Hollywood's latest release, the first-run film now available on video, or the latest sitcom episode has replaced the headlines and game scores. And, of course, the advent of the new high-tech-surround-sound-multiple-theater complexes hasn't hurt box office figures.

I am not saying that you should go out and watch movies for the express purpose of witnessing. But with the increase in theatergoers, more and more people are talking about what they have seen. They talk about the stars or the emotional scars inflicted on the characters they play. They find themselves playing the part of armchair reviewers scrutinizing plot development, identifying the presence or absence of any redeeming moral virtue. And some are predisposed to count cuss words or body parts. That gives Christians a unique opportunity to enter into discussions with unbelievers.

True, we do not always view the same films. But when we have, would you think it unnatural or intimidating to ask a neighbor or colleague what they thought of it? "What did you think the turning point was?" can easily lead to a more focused discussion in which you ask questions like, "In what way do you find yourself struggling with the issues those characters faced?" or "With whom did you most identify?"

Think about those questions in regard to what you've watched in the past year. Do you think applying them to films or TV shows might open up doors for conversation with a neighbor across the street? You know the one I mean. You wave and call him by his first name, but you've only really talked to him once since he moved in, and that was the time you simply asked what lawn fertilizer he was using.

> **If we are to follow Jesus' example, we must gain some facility with our culture's terminology.**

If we are to follow Jesus' example and learn how to speak God's truth in the language of the people, we must gain some facility with our culture's terminology. And if the media really is the language most non-Christians understand, we would do well to identify which spiritual concepts and universal values Hollywood is producing and probe those meanings. Karen Mains puts it this way:

> The influence of popular media is so pervasive in our culture and the income it generates so enormous that it is imperative for Christians to learn to use this language to tell God's stories. The church will never have this kind of money to expend on missions and outreach, but we can learn to leverage the products of Hollywood's expenditures for our own

purpose. *(From a talk entitled "Translating the Word to the World.")*

Steven Spielberg's masterful production of *Schindler's List* not only stole the Academy Award for Best Picture a few years ago, it stole my heart. I wrote about it and preached about it. Here is a secular film (with a few admittedly offensive scenes easily skipped with the fast-forward button) that powerfully illustrates the concept of salvation. It is a movie of epic proportions about a wealthy German industrialist who hid more Jews than any other Gentile during the Holocaust.

In the film, Oskar Schindler wins the favor of the Nazis and devises a plan to make use of Jewish slave labor by manufacturing mess kits for the German army. As Jews are randomly, brutally, and senselessly massacred in a Polish ghetto, Schindler protects those in his factory. All his employees are exempt from the unthinkable atrocities. In time, Schindler begins to compile a list of Jews to be added to his employee roster. To be on the list means everything. It is a matter of life and death. As long as people can prove their name is on Schindler's list, their lives are spared.

As the war escalated, Schindler eventually had to bribe the Nazis in order to continue hiding his workers. Purchasing their protection cost Schindler everything he had. Wow! In Oskar Schindler we see a reflection of our redemption. Jesus purchased our protection and salvation by giving all. In the process, he added our name to the list the Bible calls the Book of Life.

Screen Your Message

Over the past two decades, a pair of Chicago film critics became household barometers for which movies to see and which ones to miss. If Gene Siskel and Roger Ebert gave a flick "two thumbs up," there was a pretty good chance the box office attraction was worth the eight bucks to see it. I'd be the first to admit, that Siskel and Ebert's thumbs were not always aimed in the right direction. Their presuppositions about what makes for edifying content did not come from a conservative Christian bias. But what I appreciated about these critics was that they really tried to identify what works in a movie and what doesn't. They developed eyes to see what lingers beneath the surface of the dialogue. Sadly, as I was about to begin writing this book, Gene Siskel succumbed to brain cancer. I miss his voice and his thumb. Yet, because of Siskel and Ebert's impact on our generation, I am convinced the language of movies is worth learning. Frankly, I believe we each, in our own way, can be a "Siskel and Ebert" in our sphere of influence for the glory of God.

Action Step 2 in the 50-Day Adventure is a chance to test your "media as a second language" proficiency. It's called "Screen Your Message." Once during the Adventure, make plans to get together with another person, a couple, or a group. (These should be primarily non-Christian people.) If you wish, you could go to a movie or watch a show you've all been "dying to see." Or, just invite them to do something social with you. While you're together, bring up a movie, video, or show that you and your friends have seen. If you've just viewed something together, use that for your coffee-and-dessert discussion.

After asking a few open-ended questions, spend time listening. Follow up with questions that steer the conversation toward whatever spiritual images you saw in the film. Refrain from preaching. If the film you saw offended your personal standards of decency, try not to get bogged down by the profanity, sexual innuendoes, or violence. Encourage your companions to share something that bothered them about the movie as well as something they felt fingered a yawning ache in the lives of people they know. "Screen Your Message" will be a fun way to try your hand at creative evangelism. If you take the assignment seriously, you'll be building bridges with people who may not have an assurance of God's love.

Jim Abrahamson is a pastor near Duke University in Durham, North Carolina. In his academic community, he's discovered that the media is a means to connect with people who are not spiritually sensitive. Jim sees plots and character development as a way of identifying the spiritual component God has wired into every human being. He observes,

> The image of God is hard to repress in people and it will often bear witness to its presence in unexpected ways. For example, the violence, immorality, and lawlessness of many Hollywood films can be too quickly dismissed as only an example of human depravity. A more sensitive assessment may also see a desperate longing for the kingdom of God (justice, fulfillment, peace, and happiness), albeit couched in strange language. (*Lessons in Leadership,* copyright © 1999 by Randal Roberts. Kregel Publications, Grand Rapids, Mich., p. 22.)

Pastor Abrahamson has discovered ours is a culture that, for the most part, speaks the language of the cinema. The universal longing for redemption and contentment, as well as the consequences of a self-serving lifestyle, are illustrated on screen day after day.

> Just imagine the impact you could make if you started relating the truths of Scripture to what people see on screen.

Just imagine the impact you could make if you began learning the language your unchurched neighbors understand and started relating the truths of Scripture to what so many people see on screen. MGM, Paramount, Disney, and the rest of the media companies are spending billions of dollars each year to portray the plight of the human soul in bigger-than-life images. We can boycott their films and protest the fact that secular production companies don't produce biblically sound stories—or we can thank God for the unbelievable opportunities those companies provide us to communicate his Word in the language and images to which people of our generation relate. Once we begin to appreciate the power inherent in translating the gospel into the dialect of the masses, our choice will be quite obvious.

In the 1920s a nineteen-year-old by the name of Cam Townsend left Occidental College in Los Angeles for Guatemala. His goal was to sell Bibles. Once he reached his destination, he realized his goal was shortsighted. Cam did not waver in his conviction that the South Americans needed God's Word. But he quickly discovered that selling them the Bible in Spanish would not be much good to them. Even if some of them could read Spanish (and many could), the language of the Bibles he brought was not the language of their heart. It was not the language in which they dreamed or the language they taught their children. It was not the dialect of their oral traditions, traditions that shaped their identity as an indigenous people.

Cam Townsend—or Uncle Cam, as he became known—shelved his plan to sell Bibles and began a grassroots organization committed to translating the Scriptures into the maiden tongues of all the people groups in the world. He believed that if people could hear God speak in their personal tongue, they would be more inclined to respond to his grace and trust his Son as their Savior.

Now, 70-some years later, Wycliffe Bible Translators has translated over 470 New Testaments into the "heart language" of indigenous peoples around the world. It has become the largest interdenominational missionary organization, with over 6,000 translators, educators, and support staff. And what is most impressive, Uncle Cam's desire to see Bible translation employed as a means of evangelism has far outdistanced his wildest dreams.

Cam Townsend's strategy was not original. He was merely mirroring an approach that accounted for Jesus' popularity. His commitment to correspond God's Word to the heart language of the masses is just like what Jesus did. And if you learn to speak God's truth in everyday language, like The People's Choice, you will find yourself attractive to many people.

For Discussion:
1. Which of Jesus' parables is your favorite? Why?

2. If Jesus were on earth today, what common metaphors do you think he would use to convey kingdom concepts?

3. Identify a spiritual value from a movie, video, or television show you have recently seen.

4. What things do you think you should try to avoid when talking about the media with non-Christians? What do you think you should capitalize upon?

5. Who is one person (or a group of people) you might begin to do this with? Make plans to follow through!

The Kingdom to Come

A new day approaches.
A kingdom awaits.
Away with a worn
veil of tears.
The lame will leap.
The poor will feast.
The haughty
will have reason to fear.
The sick will be healthy.
The shunned will be loved.
The oppressor
will tug at his chains.
The disfigured will smile.
The heartsick will sing.
The frauder will forfeit her gains.

—gea

CHAPTER
SIX

In Search of a Sequel

MY THREE DAUGHTERS' favorite movie was made 20-some years before they were born. No matter how many times they see Disney's original *Parent Trap*, they watch it with the same interest as they did the first time they saw it. Maybe you've seen it many times, too. It's the film with Brian Keith, Maureen O'Hara, and precocious Haley Mills, who plays both a young girl and her estranged twin sister. There have been many sequels to and remakes of *The Parent Trap* over the years. But only the original one gets three thumbs up in our family.

Speaking of sequels, the original *Godfather* gave way to several subsequent efforts. *Star Trek*, too. (Or should I say *Star Trek* Nine?) *Honey, I Shrunk the Kids* was followed by *Honey, I Blew up the Kid*, which was followed by *Honey, We Shrunk Ourselves*. Even the recent remake of the '50s classic *Father of the Bride* was followed by a sequel.

Guess what? It doesn't take a film critic to claim that the first release has what those that follow behind don't.

That's true in Hollywood, and it's true of life. Case in point: Sequels in marriages. Over 50 percent of first marriages end in divorce, 75 percent of second marriages never make it, and 90 percent of third marriages crash and burn. Sad stats, right? But as sad as it is that half of all first marriages fail, at least they don't fail as often as repeat performances.

Though ours is a world where sequels can't match the coattails they ride on, it's also a world that desperately longs for a remake. The original version is a pretty sorry story. In terms of a screenwriter's description, the human story is certainly not a comedy. It's a drama more apt to be called a tragedy.

Consider the plot. Man and woman make love. Man and woman make weapons. Man and woman make war. Man and woman make a mess of the perfect world God created for his glory and their pleasure. Yes, the story of the world is a sad one:

★ Students kill their peers in Pearl, Mississippi; Paducah, Kentucky; Jonesboro, Arkansas; and Littleton, Colorado.

★ In racially based massacres in Kosovo, Serbs annihilate the Albanians and Albanians annihilate the Serbs.

★ In the United States, one in four people will contract cancer.

★ Six people are infected with the AIDS virus every minute.

★ Forty thousand people die of hunger-related causes around the world every 24 hours.

★ More than 60 percent of all boys and 40 percent of all girls in our country become sexually active before the age of fifteen.

★ More than 60 percent of people between fourteen and thirty years of age would give up food before they would give up their music.

★ Over 25 percent of clergy admit to having had inappropriate sexual contact with someone other than their spouse.

★ Only 35 percent of Americans believe that most people can be trusted.

Get the picture? Now let me paint a more attractive one.

A Better Kingdom

Imagine rolling green hills undulating upward toward a cobalt-blue sky. Brilliant red, yellow, and purple spring flowers push their petals above the unmown grass. As the warm Galileean breeze sweeps down the hillside, the flowers bow as if praying.

But the wildflowers aren't the only ones who feel the gentle wind, nor are they the only ones in a prayerful posture. Several hundred men, many with their wives, some with their children, recline in the grass, listening to a young man in his early thirties telling stories about a coming kingdom. His stories are unique. Against the backdrop of first-century Roman oppression, he depicts a better world. He describes a sequel that promises to surpass the original.

In the Sermon on the Mount (Matthew 5—7), Jesus gave a preview of coming attractions.

Over and over again he said, "You have heard it said . . . , but I say to you. . . ." In other words, it was as if Jesus were saying, "In the old days, this is what people believed to be true, but have I got good news for you!"

If you have been to the National Archives building in Washington, D. C., you've probably seen the slogan carved in the marble exterior of the grand building that houses the Declaration of Independence, the U. S. Constitution, and the Bill of Rights. It reads, "The past is but prologue to the future." In terms of coming attractions, that was how Jesus was previewing the kingdom of God. The best is yet to come!

The Gospel of Matthew provides us with an eyewitness account of this memorable message. In chapters 5, 6, and 7, Matthew provides us with a transcription of Jesus words. It all begins with that poetic litany we have come to call The Beatitudes:

Blessed are the poor in spirit,
  for theirs is the kingdom of heaven.
Blessed are those who mourn,
  for they will be comforted.
Blessed are the meek,
  for they will inherit the earth.
Blessed are those who hunger and thirst
    for righteousness,
  for they will be filled.
Blessed are the merciful,
  for they will be shown mercy.
Blessed are the pure in heart,
  for they will see God.
Blessed are the peacemakers,
  for they will be called sons of God.
Blessed are those who are persecuted
    because of righteousness,
  for theirs is the kingdom of heaven.
Blessed are you when people insult you,
persecute you and falsely say all kinds of
evil against you because of me. Rejoice
and be glad, because great is your reward
in heaven, for in the same way they persecuted the prophets who were before
you. (Matthew 5:1–12)

Did you notice that the word *beatitude* doesn't even appear in the biblical text? There's an easy explanation for that. Centuries after Jesus spoke these words, theologians gave this section a summary heading. The word *beatitude* is of Latin derivation and means "to make happy." Since the word translated "blessed" has to do with ultimate happiness, it seemed an appropriate heading.

Jesus cast a vision of a better kingdom, now and future.

Jesus envisioned a better kingdom, a kingdom of ultimate happiness, where the injustices and unfair consequences of life in a less-than-perfect, broken world will be resolved and compensated. The coming kingdom is, as a pastor friend of mine put it, where God gets what he always wanted. But at the same time, it is a kingdom where all we could ever hope has a happy ending.

As I contemplate this coming kingdom of incredible joy, I'm sitting at my word processor, struggling to write this chapter. My mind is filled with all kinds of distracting thoughts. The community in which I live is reeling from an unimaginable tragedy. A young mother, distraught at her crumbling marriage, lost touch with reality. The results have crippled our entire community.

Attempting to strike out at her husband, her twisted mind plots a way to destroy him by destroying what he treasures most. One at a time, as she puts her three children to bed, she medicates them with a drug prescribed for her depression. Once they are asleep, she returns to their bedrooms and pinches their noses and covers their mouths, suffocating them to death.

At last, rationality hits her. She realizes that in

*denying her husband the children, she has denied
herself them as well. Her subsequent suicide attempt
fails. Only when she dials 911 and reports the deaths
of her seven-year-old, six-year-old, and three-year-old
children, do the authorities converge on her 120-year-
old Victorian mansion valued at more than a million
dollars. Inside the dream home, a wedding dress lay
crumpled, and near it, a wedding photo with a knife
through her husband's heart.*

Marilyn and David Lemak's world appeared to
be perfect. He was a successful doctor, and she
was a respected nurse. They made loads of money.
They lived in Naperville, Illinois, an affluent sub-
urb west of Chicago, which had just been named
the best city with a population over a hundred
thousand in which to raise children. Their home
was the envy of the community. Their two sons
and one daughter were strikingly attractive.

**I thought of three other crosses
that stood out on a hill in a world
as ugly and depraved as the one
in which we live.**

After the tragic, bold headlines woke
Napervillians that unforgettable March morning,
I drove by the Lemak home. Three makeshift
crosses had been planted in the front yard
behind yellow plastic police tape. I thought of
three other crosses that stood out on a hill far
away, in a country far from here, in a world as
ugly and depraved as the one in which we live.

There was one for Jesus and two others for a
pair of unnamed common thieves who, like you
and me, were guilty of imperfect lives. That trio
of crossbeams reminds us that ours is a world
where sin often wins, innocent children die, jus-

THE PEOPLE'S CHOICE

tice dwindles, natural disasters and wars level the castles of our dreams, power pins love to the mat, forgiveness is misunderstood, and even God himself is judged a criminal and sentenced to die.

But while ours is a world that smells of death and decay more often than it smells of abundant life, the Cross is a hopeful symbol. Through it, we see that in such a broken world, God weeps with us. He is a loving King who still holds the reigns, even when he does not hold back the showers of suffering. He is a God who reluctantly allows evil to stalk the earth in order to preserve a world in which individuals are not cosmic puppets. Jesus' brief appearance on planet earth was not just to assure us that God understands our wicked world. He also brought hope for change. By denying his divine nature and taking on humanity, Jesus announced in no uncertain terms that a remake was in the works.

At the beginning of every spring, we approach the horizon of Easter. During the 40-day period many churches refer to as Lent, we take a sobering journey on an uphill path that leads to Resurrection Sunday. It's a season of penitence, self-denial, and reflection, in which we are called to remember the suffering of Jesus that resulted in our salvation. During this purposeful pilgrimage to the open tomb, we discover all over again that those three ancient crosses are not the final mileposts on our somber journey. They will be dwarfed by an empty tomb.

In other words, no matter how many crucifixions we are called to face, despair is not the final chapter—grace is! No wonder the biography of Jesus Christ, written in the blood of irrational tragedy, is called "Good News." God's love can't be silenced. And even though the kingdom Jesus

promised in the Sermon on the Mount still
awaits, we won't have to wait for it forever.

The Kingdom Here and Now

If you look carefully at what Jesus taught on the
mountaintop, you'll see that his vision for a better kingdom wasn't all futuristic. Portions of the
Sermon on the Mount have to do with the here
and now, not just the there and later. In this same
chapter, Jesus goes on record saying that we who
walk in his footprints are the salt of the earth and
the light of the world. Not in the sweet by and
by, not somewhere over the rainbow, but right
where we are in sweet and sour present tense
where tensions run high and morality runs low.

As Jesus intimated, the presence of Christians
in the world is making a difference for good, no
matter how bad the headlines of the morning
newspaper may be. Thank God for people who
are willing live that kingdom on earth right now:

★ Those who peaceably advocate the
  rights of the unborn
★ Families who provide room and board
  for young women caught in the dilemma of unplanned pregnancies
★ People who walk the hallways of AIDS
  units offering compassion and hope,
  without judgment, in Jesus' name
★ Nurses who seek out opportunities as
  hospice workers
★ Professional and lay ministers who
  befriend prisoners
★ Christians who willingly wade through
  the muddy waters of politics to stand
  up for those who can't
★ Volunteers at homeless shelters

- ★ Those who help refugees recover from unthinkable disaster
- ★ Christian teachers in public schools
- ★ Reporters who hold biblical convictions in the media
- ★ Christian screenwriters in Hollywood

As followers of Jesus, these and many others are the salt of the earth. They are the light of the world. And you are one of them! Because of what Jesus taught on one hill far away, and because of what he sacrificed on another, his vision of a better kingdom is already making an impact.

In spite of the hatred, immorality, and suffering there is in our world, have you ever thought of what it would be like if Jesus had never been born? As with the leavening influence of yeast in bread, the life of Jesus has raised the standard of life and morality over the past 2,000 years. His Golden Rule is the standard by which even the non-religious evaluate appropriate behavior. His example of compassion and mercy is the hallmark of heroism, as illustrated by the popularity of such cultural icons as Mother Teresa, Princess Diana, and Oskar Schindler. The church Christ founded contributed to the schools, hospitals, publishing, music, art, and international dialogue of current civilization.

Through the church, Jesus has also given us a glimpse of what the kingdom of God will look like "when we all get to heaven." The church is a tangible expression of heaven's agenda. It's not a perfect picture, but it is recognizable.

Many churches refer to the place where God's people gather for worship as the *sanctuary*. I like that term. The church I grew up in called it the *auditorium*. It wasn't until I went away to a

Christian college that I heard of a sanctuary. Somehow the word *sanctuary* better serves what goes on in the place where we offer ourselves to God. In Latin, the root word means "set apart." A sanctuary is sacred space, holy ground. It's a special place. Even our contemporary, secular use of the word *sanctuary* suggests a protective refuge. It's a harbinger of safety.

> **The church is a tangible
> expression of heaven's agenda.
> It's not a perfect picture,
> but it is recognizable.**

But beyond the sense of comfort we derive from a stained-glass room in the church, we Christians offer sanctuary to a world still waiting for the kingdom of God to come in all its glory. In Christ's company of believers, others ache with us when we ache. They bury our loved ones and bear our burdens while carrying us on the wings of prayer when we find it impossible to pray. We're a community of halo-less saints who, because we know we have sinned, are more inclined to accept others just as they are. In the church we see what Jesus anticipated when he spoke of a world in which God's will would be done on earth just as it is in heaven.

Do you relate to what I'm saying? Let me try sketching it another way. People in first-century Palestine saw in Jesus the first fruits of a harvest of righteousness, justice, and mercy for which they had longed since the garden variety of Eden's crops stopped growing. Jesus' vision for a better world was a source of wonder to them. Any church that articulates and animates his message remains a source of wonder to a skeptical, self-absorbed culture. (By the way, here's a new way to define *wonder*: Wonder is whatever causes you to open your mouth and say "awe" without being asked by a doctor!)

The church where Dwight and Aileen Hawley are members is one such place. Jesus is not just celebrated in the words of praise choruses projected on a screen in Sunday morning worship. He is honored in the way his followers live out his words between Sundays. At Wheaton Bible Church in suburban Chicago, you can glimpse a sneak preview of heaven.

I work with Dwight. In addition to being our office web master, he is our "go to" guy. When anyone has a computer problem, they "go to" Dwight. We're all sure he can fix anything and answer any computer question. But there's one thing Dwight can't easily fix, one question he can't answer. It's the problem cancer poses in the life of Aileen, his wife.

Aileen not only lost her business once the cancer cells became mercilessly aggressive—she also lost her leg. Chemotherapy continues after the unexpected amputation. But so do the tangible expressions of love and concern that flow from Dwight and Aileen's Sunday school class at Wheaton Bible Church. They provide meals several times a week, and they creatively raise money to defray the mounting unreimbursed doctor's bills that will soon rival Mount Everest. Members of the church are also remodeling the Hawley home to make it wheelchair accessible.

Do you have to wait until you pass the city limit signs of heaven before the kingdom of Jesus kicks in? Dwight and Aileen would say no! This week's Adventure theme celebrates what they understand: A better world in the future . . . and now! And because Jesus is at work in his church, the better world that's a-comin' is in part already here.

Glimpsing the Future

Contemplating the difference the life of Jesus has made in our world reminds me of Frank Capra's classic Christmas movie, *It's a Wonderful Life.* George Bailey, having given himself unselfishly to serve others, finds himself in the middle of a financial nightmare—the victim of his uncle's irresponsibility. While contemplating suicide, George encounters the guardian angel assigned to him. In his recitation of all that has gone wrong, George exclaims, "I wish I'd never been born!"

Clarence the angel seizes on the wish as a teachable moment. He takes George back into a world deprived of his existence. It is a dark and cruel world, bereft of the joy and significance George would have provided. Finally, Clarence gets his despondent disciple to see how his life has impacted others and just how wonderful his life is after all.

If it's been a while since you've watched *It's A Wonderful Life,* why not rent it and view it from the perspective of how God uses the little events of our lives to impact others in our family, our church, our community, and, ultimately, our world? As you watch it, take note of how the George Bailey character models celebrating people. He's a master at finding legitimate reasons to compliment someone. He knows how to make the little guy feel important.

So, how are you doing with Action Step 3? One of the ways Jesus cast a vision of a better kingdom was by helping people glimpse their potential. What a fun assignment we've been given, to do something every day that elevates another person's sense of worth! As difficult and depressing as our world can be, each of us has been given a wonderful life. When we take time to write an encouraging note, greet a stranger on the street with a smile, compliment the clerk on his or her sweater, they may be more inclined to believe today is a gift from a loving God who has a better kingdom in store for them.

Do you remember my mention of my Filipino neighbor whose daughter gave birth to a child out of wedlock (chapter 2)? Well, this week I found a way to "celebrate" not only Meli but her granddaughter, Phoenix. When I saw the proud grandma and baby out in the front yard, I ran for my camera and walked across the street. "Let me take some pictures of little Phoenix," I offered. Meli smiled her approval.

The snapshots turned out great. I scrawled a little note expressing my appreciation to Meli and tucked the photos in an envelope. When I knew the mail carrier had left her mail, I sneaked over to the mailbox and added my card to the pile. Easy? You bet it was. And fun, too. This world is a better kingdom when your faith not only invites you to bring joy to others but gives you permission to have fun in the process.

All the same, the kingdom Jesus promised is yet to be fully realized. The world is not as bad as it could be, but it's bad enough. The sequel for which we long seems too long in the making. In the meantime, we live in a world where "we see through a glass, darkly" (1 Corinthians 13:12, KJV). That's how the apostle Paul referred to our less-than-perfect existence.

What do you think of when you hear those words? I think of those eighteenth-century windows I've seen at Old Sturbridge Village in Massachusetts. The panes of those vintage, Revolutionary War buildings are thick and uneven, yielding a distorted view of the outside. But the windows aren't the problem in our case. What Paul describes is not inferior glass as much as the pain of living in an imperfect world. True, our ability to make sense of what we see is impaired by what we have to look through. But the real problem is what is on the other side of the inferior windows. The world we attempt to focus on is a world of shadows. C. S. Lewis called it "Shadowlands."

> **What Paul describes is not inferior glass as much as the pain of living in an imperfect world.**

A movie called *Shadowlands* was released in 1996. It told the fascinating, albeit tragic, love story of Clive Staples Lewis, the renowned Oxford professor, and his American pen pal, Joy Davidman. Although the critics did not give *Shadowlands* the attention it deserved, millions of moviegoers were exposed for the first time to the author of The Chronicles of Narnia, who was one of the twentieth century's most brilliant minds. They also saw a fairly accurate portrayal of how faith sustained a middle-aged man as he watched his beloved bride slowly succumb to the ravages of terminal cancer.

Anthony Hopkins played a convincing Lewis who is not incapable of questioning God or beyond displaying anger. Here is an honest believer who admits to doubts and yet tenaciously holds on to his conviction that suffering is not meaningless and death is not final. For Lewis, hardship is the megaphone God uses to get our attention and by which he reminds us the kingdom of heaven is not fully come. Death is but the passageway into a Narnia-like eternity where our present land of shadows gives way to a reality of life lived entirely out in the open and in the light of God's loving countenance.

The cinematic beauty of the film is enhanced by a musical soundtrack that offers appropriate melodic shading for each scene. But the true beauty of *Shadowlands* for me is not the cinematography or musical score. It is the portrait of genuine faith that grows from intellectual confidence to experiential certainty. It is a profile of a Christian in process, who has no choice but to accept the reality of living in a land dominated by the shadows of disappointment and death. With his acceptance comes insight and the ability to see beyond the ugliness of cancer, depression, death, and lingering sorrow to the face of God and the grace of immortality that still awaits us.

In the shadows of my imagination, I journey back to the night before Christ offered his life as collateral for the coming kingdom.

He is there in that dark, upper room. The air is heavy with candle smoke and the heat from sweaty bodies leaning together at a common table. Their bellies are full. Their feet are clean (thanks to Jesus). But their hearts are empty. The atmosphere is eerie. The aroma of roasted lamb is mingled with the scent of approaching doom. They can't quite make sense of it all. Jesus, sensing their apprehension and confusion, attempts to calm their fears.

"Do not let your hearts be troubled," he says. "Trust in God; trust also in me. In my Father's house are many rooms. . . . I am going there to prepare a place for you" (John 14:1–2).

Do you hear Jesus? He was talking kingdom talk. Father's house. Many rooms. It's future! The kingdom is still somewhere out there. But he hastened to add that the kingdom was also there with them, in that familiar upper room, in the approaching gloomy weekend, and wherever they went until he comes for them. In that same section of John's Gospel, Jesus reminded them that prior to "mansion-time" they would have mansion-sized problems: "In this world you will have trouble." Yet, note what he said in the same breath. "But take heart! I have overcome the world" (John 16:33).

Now, not then. Now, not future. The kingdom had already broken into their lives—and into ours, too—this side of the end of it all. Because Jesus has overcome the world, the flesh, and the devil, and because of the peace he has made possible through his Holy Spirit, even our existence this side of heaven is a better place than it was before he came.

A Valid Vision

Those who observe the church from a distance aren't looking for a perfect place or a sinless people. They are too intelligent to think perfection is really possible on a defective planet whose warranty has already run out. Rather, what they hope to find is the "DNA" of Jesus in those who claim to be his followers. They are looking for a church that doesn't just advertise faith, hope, and love, but one that delivers. Does yours? People are looking for a congregation that lives out what Jesus promised, instead of what the deacons passed at their last meeting by a vote of 12–10. They're looking for a little peace of heaven on earth, where the mystery of another world

pins the predictable routines of self-absorbed culture to the mat.

I saw that peace in the lives of two people I
had the privilege of pastoring. Their moving
story is living proof that what Jesus saw in his
vision of a better world was not a daydream or
just a reward reserved for heaven.

Linda had known the bitterness of a sweet life
gone sour. Her storybook romance with Steve had
missing pages. Even though they loved their jobs
as teachers and Young Life volunteers at the same
California high school, they were not able to con-
ceive. The facts were a test of their sincere faith.

Swallowing their disappointment, they proceeded to adopt a baby. Because of their love for
children, they adopted four more. Life was good,
the house was full, but it was not without challenges. Steve developed kidney disease and eventually required dialysis. In a necessary transfusion,
the unthinkable occurred: Steve was infected with
the HIV virus and died after an agonizing battle
with AIDS.

At forty-two years of age, Linda was left with
a broken heart and five children under ten. Her
faith, her family, and her church sustained her as
she picked up the shards of her shattered dreams.
She knew there could be no sequel to the special
marriage she and Steve had. But within a couple
years, Linda longed for companionship and a
partner who would help her raise Michael, Peter,
Laura, Nathanael, and Emily.

I once heard Linda confess her chance of
landing a man was less than of being kidnapped
by a Middle Eastern terrorist. After all, who would
want a woman approaching fifty with five kids?

Enter a guy by the name of Larry. Larry was a
recovering alcoholic in his middle forties who,

five years earlier, had lost his job, his family, and any hope of salvaging the rest of his life. His world literally collapsed. In the gutter of self pity, Larry lay helpless.

Though he had hit bottom, he had yet to hit his stride. Christians from a local church embraced Larry with tough love and tender forgiveness. They gave him hope. Larry surrendered to the lordship of Jesus Christ and began to devour God's Word with the same thirst he had approached the bottle.

When Larry's path intersected Linda's, a new trail emerged on God's sovereign map. The recovered drunk not only welcomed this beautiful widow into his life, he adored her children.

Would it surprise you if I told you that within three years of their wedding, Larry and Linda and their children were accepted as missionaries with Wycliffe Bible Translators? In the remote regions of Colombia and the Wycliffe Center in North Carolina, this family is engaged in dubbing films into indigenous languages of unreached Latin American people groups.

Unbelievable? Call it a miracle, if you wish. But I choose to think of Linda and Larry's life together as just one example among countless others that validate the vision Jesus cast. Under his kingship, the Father's kingdom not only will come, but has come, and his will is being done on earth as it is in heaven.

Discussion Questions:

1. Think about your own life. How do you think your world would be different if you had never been born?

2. What is it about the dream of a better kingdom that captures the attention of the masses?

3. What do you find most difficult about Action Step 3, "Celebrate People?" What might that challenge reveal about you?

4. How do you see the "Shadowlands" playing themselves out in your life? How does your faith bring you hope, despite these difficulties?

5. What are some ways you can help others see the kingdom of God here on earth?

A Faithful Finish

When God calls,
a gun sounds,
and a marathon begins.
A lifetime of measured steps
which,
because of the distance to be covered,
takes in stride
the potholes along the way.
Disappointment.
Tears.
Rejection.
Exhaustion.
Failure.
Loss.
A cross, I think He called it.
The one who finished first,
who near the end
of His long distance race
(though winded)
sighed, "I thirst!"
It was what He saw
beyond the finish line
that gave Him courage
to stay His course.
A faithful finish
and a Father's proud
"Well done!"

—gea

CHAPTER
SEVEN

That's a Wrap!

THE OLYMPIC FLAME BLAZED BRIGHTLY as the autumn sun began to set. The date was October 20, 1968. A capacity crowd at the Olympic stadium in Mexico City had just witnessed a memorable moment. Mamo Waldi of Ethiopia had crossed the finish line, having completed all 26 miles, 385 yards of the Olympic marathon before anyone else. He looked as strong and as vigorous as when he had started. Within an hour and a half, the other runners had completed the grueling course, moving to the first aid stations that had been set up on the stadium infield.

As darkness drew near, the stadium lights illuminated the emptying grandstands. There was no need to hang around. Attendees had just witnessed the last event of the day. And then, a siren blew. There were whistles, police cars, and the accompanying commotion at the entrance to the track. All remaining eyes focused on a young man who stumbled into view, dressed in the colors of Tanzania.

John Steven Aquari had fallen early in the race but, after receiving first aid, continued to push through the pain and kept running. Obviously injured, the last and almost forgotten marathon runner limped his remaining mandatory lap around the track, his leg wrapped in a bloodied bandage. He was greeted by a standing ovation and a reporter who asked, "Why didn't you quit? It's obvious you're injured. Why didn't you just give up?"

With quiet dignity the exhausted athlete replied, "My country didn't send me seven thousand miles to start this race. My country sent me to finish!"

That is the kind of determined resolve it takes to complete a mission that burns like a fire in your soul. Hear the same kind of conviction in a prayer Sir Francis Drake wrote centuries ago: "O Lord, when you give to your servants to endeavor any great matter, grant us also to know that this is not the beginning, but the continuing of the same, until it be thoroughly finished which yields the true glory. Through Him, who for the finishing of Your work, laid down his life."

A big part of what made Jesus The People's Choice was the courage he displayed in going the distance. He stayed the course. Though tempted to quit, when he hit the wall of discouragement and spiritual despair, he bounced off and kept on. Because of the energizing power of the Holy Spirit and his ongoing connectedness to the Father, Jesus modeled the necessary courage it takes to accomplish a vital mission.

The Courage of a Winner

At another public gathering 2,000 years before the Olympic stadium event in Mexico City, the crowds in Jerusalem lined another marathon course. Unlike the long-distance foot race, the marathon I have in mind is a human's race with a spiritual goal. This marathon had lasted 33 years, but at last the end was in sight. The crowds cheered as the lone contestant entered into view.

He was riding a donkey. He smiled and waved at children who called his name: "Jesus!" Others shouted out, "Hosanna!" and "Blessed is he who comes in the name of the Lord!" In a spirit of celebration, those welcoming the rabbi waved palm branches. In one voice they spurred on The People's Choice, unaware of what awaited him at the finish line. Like John Steven Aquari, he would be bloodied and wounded when he reached the end.

The Palm Sunday procession finished at the temple mount. Dismounting from his donkey, Jesus took in the disconcerting scene. His Father's house of prayer and worship had disintegrated into a marketplace of superficial religious trinkets. Then, he turned around and walked away, turned off by what he saw. He refused to spoil the spirit of celebration that inaugurated his final journey to Jerusalem.

The next day, Jesus returned to the temple with spring cleaning on his mind. Overruling objections, he overturned tables, sending pigeons and coins flying. The gentle Jesus, meek and mild, who was known to carry toddlers in his arms, proved he is capable of another persona. With cutting words, he sliced through the arrogant atmosphere populated by self-righteous merchants. Angrily, Jesus cleaned house. Courageously, he took a stand—all the while knowing he would be misunderstood.

I can remember the first time I was called upon to take a stand I knew I would be unpopular with more than a few. It was my first church. I'd been out of seminary only a few months. I knew that one of the couples who attended worship on a regular basis was not married, even though the attendance registration slips indicated they lived at the same address. As long as they didn't apply for membership, I figured I had plenty of time to broach the subject. I was wrong.

In the process of having family portraits taken to compile a church pictorial directory, John and Karen were insistent that they have their picture taken together as a family unit, complete with a listing of their address. I can still remember the knot in my stomach while driving to visit with them in their home. As I knocked on the door, my knees knocked, too. With every ounce of courage I could muster, I informed John and Karen that it would not be possible for us to include them as a couple. To do so, I said, would imply that we endorsed cohabitation as an acceptable lifestyle.

Feeling like my mouth was lined with cotton, I went on to say that I'd love to do pre-marital counseling with them and schedule a date on the church calendar when they could be married. They graciously accepted my position and agreed to be photographed individually. Within two years' time, I stood with them as another photographer took their wedding portrait.

Jesus courageously completed his assigned mission.

Now, granted, the courage I pulled together for my one-man mission to John and Karen's home doesn't begin to compare with the courage Jesus demonstrated when pointing his finger at those in the temple who thumbed their noses at him. But it reminded me just how easy it would be to avoid conflict and compromise commitments. It also reminded me what a courageous man Jesus was.

Our first glimpse into the courageous instinct of Jesus is on a day when two parents discovered their twelve-year-old son was missing. The annual festival in Jerusalem had ended. A large group of families, traveling together to Nazareth, was halfway through their three-day trek on foot. Because of the groupings, one young mother wasn't all that concerned that her eldest son hadn't been seen since they'd left the city. She and her husband, a middle-aged carpenter, may have been bringing up the rear. Perhaps he couldn't walk as fast as he used to. Besides, there were other children who required being carried. So Mary and Joseph assumed that Jesus was up ahead with his cousins and friends. But as word filtered back from the front of the pack, a lack of concern crescendoed into full-fledged fear. Jesus was missing!

Mary quickly distributed the younger children with adults in their caravan. Together with Joseph, she turned toward Jerusalem and began to retrace a day's worth of steps in haste.

Breathlessly, she ran ahead of her older husband. Eventually, her feet slowed down, but her heart continued to race. Finally, in total exhaustion, they reached their destination. Asking on random street corners if anyone had seen a lost boy, they were told there was a precocious lad in the temple area, talking with the elders. They pushed their way through the crowd of pilgrims continuing to exit the city and came upon young Jesus. Their alarming reaction took him by surprise, which, in turn, took Mary and Joseph by surprise: "Didn't you know I had to be in my Father's house?" (Luke 2:49).

His courage, his conviction, his sense of purpose—it's all there. From the beginning of his adolescence to his final breath on a Roman cross,

Jesus was resolute. His Father did not send him across the ocean of eternity to simply *begin* the marathon of redemption for a fallen race but to *finish* it.

Do you recall how Luke describes Jesus' determination to finish his God-ordained course? "He steadfastly set his face to go to Jerusalem" (Luke 9:51, KJV). The disciples were amazed. They were afraid of what was to come, even though they didn't fully understand Jesus' prediction of his death. But the courage they saw Jesus draw upon captured their imagination and, in time, motivated their own martyrdom. It wasn't his courage alone. It was also the outcome his courage accomplished.

If you've ever walked the slope of the Mount of Olives toward the eastern gate of Jerusalem's Old City, no doubt you ventured into the Garden of Gethsamane. Once inside the wrought-iron fence, you stood before an olive grove of old gnarled and twisted trees that date back to the time of Jesus. It's amazing! Both times I've had the privilege of leading tour groups into this famous garden, I've stopped and reflected on the courage that pulsated in a very brave heart.

I know I would have given up, hands down! I'm a descendent of Peter the chicken heart.

In my mind's eye, I see Jesus lying prostrate on the ground in the shadow of these same trees. Overwhelmed by what's in store both physically and spiritually, his fearlessness flags momentarily. He pleads with his Father for a way out. He agonizes. He perspires. Sadly, he turns and looks over his shoulder to see his sleeping friends too tired

to pray with him. Talk about a solitary confine-
ment of the soul; Jesus is nearly ready to bail out
and give in.

I know I would have given up, hands down!
I'm a descendent of Peter the chicken heart.
Good old Simon Peter: "You gotta believe me,
Jesus. I'm the brave one. Even if all of these other
so-called disciples of yours turn tail and run, I
never will. You've got my word on that, Jesus.
Trust me this time, Lord." Oh, how he crowed.
But when it was the rooster's turn to cackle out
reveille, Peter ended up having to eat crow. Yes, I
would tend to be like Peter. Ironically, on my last
visit to the Garden of Gethsamane, I saw a stray
rooster perched near the olive trees. It was a
silent reminder to me of the ever-present danger
of surrendering my goals to my fears.

It would have been easy for Jesus to cave in
and quit. But, he didn't! In the end, he squelched
his doubts and stared down his fears. He stood
up straight, squared his shoulders, and shoul-
dered his cross. Alone, he bravely stumbled forward on the inclined path to a hill we call
Calvary. He had to. It was the only trail that
leads to our salvation. And he knew it.

Jesus' example of remarkable courage attracted more than the godly. Even pagans were
impressed. I think of Pontius Pilate. After observing the inhumane treatment and bloody abuse
Jesus underwent at the hands of his soldiers,
Pilate marveled at the victim's resolve not to back
away from his claim to be the Son of God.
Against the backdrop of the religious elite calling
for Jesus' execution, the Roman governor found
no fault in Jesus. He went so far as to wash his
hands of what continued to unfold before him.
What Pilate himself lacked in moral strength and

political courage, he could see in the One he
allowed to be crucified by default.

And don't forget the Roman centurion.
Remember him? He's the one who stood at the
foot of the cross. Having witnessed the torment-
ed, dying Jesus offer compassion to his grieving
mother, assurance to a repentant thief being crucified next to him, and blanket forgiveness to
those who had nailed him to a tree, the centurion scratched his head in utter amazement. How
could one so weak seek the good of others amidst
excruciating pain? The soldier's wonder succumbed to God-instilled insight as he verbalized
unlearned faith: "Surely this man was the Son of
God!" (Mark 15:39).

Obviously, Jesus is in a category all his own.
But when we think of him as The People's
Choice, we can also think of other icons of literary fame. The classical heroes and champions
depicted in the Great Books collection have three
characteristics in common: They are capable of
feats that are beyond the ability of ordinary men.
They die at home in seasons of isolation, removed
from their peers. And they demonstrate incredible
courage.

In the case of Jesus, we see the incarnation of
all three qualities. And to think—he was no legend. The People's Choice lived and breathed and
bravely bore his cross. There's just something
about bare-knuckled bravery that we respond to,
isn't there?

Holding On for Dear Life

On a commuter flight from Portland, Maine, to
Boston in the summer of 1987, the pilot heard
an unusual noise near the rear of the aircraft.
Henry Dempsey turned the controls over to his

co-pilot and went back to check it out. As he reached the tail section, the plane hit an air pocket, and Dempsey was tossed against the rear door. He quickly discovered the source of the mysterious noise. The rear door had not been properly latched before takeoff, and it fell open. Dempsey was instantly sucked out of the jet.

The co-pilot, seeing the red light on the control panel that indicated an open door, radioed the nearest airport requesting permission to make an emergency landing. He reported that Dempsey had fallen out of the plane and requested that a helicopter be dispatched to search that area of the ocean.

After the plane had landed, the ground crew found Henry Dempsey holding onto the outdoor ladder of the aircraft. Somehow, he had caught the ladder and managed to hold on for ten minutes as the plane flew 200 miles per hour at an altitude of 4,000 feet. What's more, as the plane made its approach and landed, Dempsey had kept his head from hitting the runway, a mere 12 inches away. According to news reports, it took several airport personnel more than a few minutes to pry the pilot's fingers free from the ladder.

When was the last time you were forced to strap on your seatbelt and hold on for dear life?

When was the last time you were forced to strap on your seatbelt and hold on for dear life as unplanned circumstances took you on a frightful ride? When was the last time you faced the temptation to cash it in and surrender a dream you believed God had planted in your heart? For some good friends of mine, it was October of 1980.

Hugh and Norma Steven waited nervously in a hospital corridor. A doctor eventually approached and greeted them with words they were not expecting. "If you're praying people, you'd better give it your best shot. We've given it ours, and it's not enough. We're losing your daughter. Wendy's will to live will determine whether or not she pulls through."

This attractive twenty-eight-year-old, single schoolteacher had checked into the hospital a few weeks earlier to have a cyst near her eye removed. Because of the location of the cyst, the doctor doubled the dose of the antibiotic he'd prescribed for the outpatient procedure to guard against any infection that might spread to the brain. Little did he know that Wendy was deathly allergic to that drug. In the days that followed her minor surgery, Wendy began to feel lethargic and experienced difficulty breathing. Her parents insisted that she move home so they could care for her.

And then came that fateful Saturday morning. Within hours of being admitted to Western Medical Center in Tustin, California, Wendy went into anaphylactic shock. Her lungs collapsed. She was connected to tubes and wires in an effort to sustain life. Barring a miracle, Wendy Steven would die. The doctor's unexpected diagnosis focused her parents' fear while galvanizing their faith.

As missionaries, the Stevens spared no time activating a worldwide prayer network. Members of Trinity Presbyterian Church, the church the family was attending in nearby Santa Ana, prayed. Friends and family dropped by the hospital to wait with Hugh and Norma. George Munzing, Trinity's pastor, and Wendy's older brother, Dave, stood at her bedside whispering words of hope and encouragement. Her unresponsiveness did not deter their efforts. Still, they didn't know if she even heard them.

She did. Wendy determined to live. With every ounce of strength and courage she could muster, she fought the temptation to give up. She saw the odds as the enemy and battled on. Through the grace of God, the miracle thousands had prayed and hoped for occurred. Within a couple of days, her condition stabilized. Within two and a half weeks, Wendy was home.

I know that story as if it were my own, because, in a way, it is. A year and a half after Wendy was released from the hospital, I stood before her pastor and her parents and six hundred other people and pledged to love her for better or for worse, for richer or for poorer, in joy and in sorrow, in sickness and in health . . . as long as we both shall live.

Wendy sensed deep in her spirit that she had a mission in life that she had not completed at the tender age of twenty-eight. Courageously, she trusted God, all the while wondering what his plans for her life might include. Well, 17 years later, they include a husband and three incredibly wonderful daughters named Kristin, Allison, and Lauren Star. Although Wendy's mission in life is far from over (God willing), she has determined to not quit when challenges come—and come they do—to our marriage, our ministry, and our frightening role as parents of impressionable teenage girls being imprinted by the values of an immoral culture.

Knowing Your Mission

As you consider your particular plight in life right now, what commitments have you verbalized that seem as far away as the finish line of a marathon race? Is it a vow you made to be faithful to your mate? Perhaps it relates to your work and paying the price integrity and honesty demand in a setting where those who cheat beat the odds of advancement. Maybe it has to do with that gnawing urge you felt as a younger person to abandon a lucrative career in order to serve Christ in ministry. Possibly it has to do with your responsibility to aging parents whose quality of life is jeopardized because you live far away from them. Could it be a commitment you made to one of your children that seemed so doable then, but so inconvenient now? In all honesty, as you face the uphill climb, you know that it will require Christlike courage to make good on those commitments.

But hear the good news: The gospel truth is that the courage Christ mustered is available to hotdog disciples like us. Imperfect, unfaithful, Peter-like in our unrealistic appraisal of our devotion, we nonetheless are candidates for the courage Christ embodied. Scripture tells us the Spirit who enabled him to deny himself and die on a cross was the same Spirit who empowered him to defeat death and exit the grave. And get this—it is the same Spirit who lives in all who have surrendered to his lordship by simple faith: "The Spirit of him who raised Jesus from the dead is living in you" (Romans 8:11).

Polyanna thinking? Pie in the sky? Nope! There is more than meringue here. You've seen the kind of practical courage I'm talking about in the lives of people you know.

Just as the masses were strangely attracted to Jesus' courageous perseverance, the onlooking, unchurched world responds to congregations that model tenacious boldness. What makes Jesus attractive to so many evokes the same response when the Body of Christ knows its mission and refuses to compromise its call. For example:

★ The church in Florida that bravely resisted the gravitational pull of "tradition." You know what I mean. The weekly call to worship begins, "As it was and ever shall be, we've always done church this way." This church began a contemporary service on Saturday night. Much to the amazement of the pessimists, the new service is thriving. Nearly a hundred people who were previously unchurched have begun coming on a regular basis in the first four months.

★ A church in Illinois that opens its fellowship hall each Thursday evening to feed the homeless a hot meal, then rolls out sleeping mats on the hardwood floor to soften their plight. Countering the criticism of those who turn up their noses (as they plug them) at the Thursday night "congregation" takes uncompromising courage.

★ One Los Angeles congregation that recently recognized the radically changing demographics of the neighborhood in which it was located. Rather than fleeing to the suburbs, the dwindling membership courageously chose to close its doors and sell their buildings to commercial developers. With the proceeds from the transaction, the church that willingly chose to die generously gave its life to plant a

Hispanic church and Latin Bible Institute across town. What's more, it was also able to establish a half-million dollar endowment for the new school.

★ The church outside Dayton, Ohio, that has carefully articulated a mission statement that requires cultural relevance in every area of ministry they attempt. Unless a suggested idea can pass through the "mission" grid, it is never cleared to be put into practice.

★ A congregation near San Francisco that recognized the need to invest in the longevity of their middle-aged pastor. By offering him a three-month sabbatical for physical rest and educational refreshment, they enabled a forty-something pastor on the verge of burnout to replenish his spiritual reservoir and keep going strong. But, as you might imagine, the resolution to grant a 12-week leave with pay was not endorsed unanimously! That's gutsy courage.

Churches that dare to live out what they believe God is calling them to do make a positive impact on the communities in which they minister. Even people who don't ever attend know there is something about those churches that is worth noting.

Is your church one of those? And how are you personally contributing to that? Is *courage* a word you would use to describe what it takes to live out your local mission?

Displays of Courage

Hundreds of thousands of junior and senior high
school students brave the elements and the
insults of their peers to gather at the flagpole outside their schools to pray for their friends, their
teachers, and their community. These daring
Christian kids are aware of a mission to reach
their world for Christ and have been empowered
to stand up for him unashamedly.

More and more students on high school and
college campuses are voluntarily signing a pledge
to wait to have sex until they are married. In our
sex-dominated culture, you know that takes
courage—not only to sign a card, but to honor
the signature.

A million men chose to stand in the gap on
behalf of righteousness in our nation. Maybe you
were there in Washington, D. C., in the fall of
1997. Yes, it took courage to go on record standing before God and repenting of personal sin. It
was quite a mission to undertake, pledging to be
husbands, fathers, and sons who would begin to
aggressively tackle the sumo sins of pornography,
workaholism, and idolatry that tend to take them
down.

We see courage displayed in those who bravely accept the death sentence of a doctor's diagnosis and spend their final months of life bearing
witness to the faithfulness of a loving God
instead of questioning his sovereign purposes for
their life. What a statement to make to a younger
generation, which deifies youth, beauty, health,
and immortality. When a committed Christian
gracefully faces difficulty and death with courage
and verbalized faith, our preoccupation with the
first 70 years of eternity is called into question.

A Long Obedience in the Same Direction may be

the title of a best-selling Christian book, but for
Dan Stocker, they are words that describe his walk
with God and a bike ride he will never forget.

In his 45 years of life, this structural engineer
from Portland, Oregon, has battled Hodgkin's disease, a triple coronary bypass, blood clots, kidney
stones, a ruptured disk, and the removal of both
his spleen and gall bladder. Although he's learned
that following Jesus doesn't necessarily mean a life
of health, wealth, and prosperity, his uphill climb
has not been without camouflaged blessings.

Here is a 6' 8" guy—with silver hair, a gray
beard, and a broad smile—who loves life and has
an incredibly big heart for kids. But Dan's health
issues presented a major obstacle to being able to
focus his love on children of his own.

> **To someone who had faced
> tougher odds before, 50 days of
> pushing pedals was just another
> milepost in his long-distance faith.**

"In 1979, when I undergoing chemotherapy
for cancer, our first child, Jason, turned two,"
Stocker recalls. "My wife, Kathie, and I wanted to
have a second child, but the treatments left me
sterile."

Their initial disappointment gave way to a confidence that God could answer their prayers for
children as he had for health issues. After Dan had
remained "cancer-free" for five years, the Stockers
began the process of adopting a child through Holt
International Children's Services. In 1986, they
received a beautiful, healthy, four-month-old,
South Korean baby girl they named Jennifer.

Then, God got his attention, Stocker says. "I
was overwhelmed by how much the Lord had

used my family to provide a constant source of support and love. But I was also convicted that there were thousands of children with special needs around the world that did not have a loving family."

What emerged was a dream as big as he is—a 3,700-mile bicycle trek from Portland, Oregon, to Portland, Maine! To someone who had faced tougher odds before, 50 days of pushing pedals was not an impossible dream. It was just another milepost in his long-distance faith.

After triple coronary bypass surgery in 1992, Dan was forced into a lifestyle change. He began riding his bike and discovered a love for cycling. One year later, Dan completed a 470-mile bicycle tour of the Oregon Trail. Stocker recalls, "As I rode, it dawned on me . . . if I could do that, why couldn't I bike my way across America to give hope to kids who might not otherwise have a chance for a normal life?"

On August 12, 1996, he left Rose City to the cheers of colleagues, neighbors, and members of his church. At the end of each day's ride, Dan called his wife with updates. Along the way, he lodged with friends and families who had adopted children through Holt International Children Services.

Although braving wind, inclement weather, and a tender posterior, Dan averaged 84 miles a day. Though he was hampered by grasshoppers in Wyoming, frogs in South Dakota, and butterflies in Minnesota, Dan admits he was "blown away" by the goodness and generosity of people all along the way who showed up to urge him on.

Dan ended his 17-state cross-country marathon on September 30. When all the pledges were totaled and paid, more than $9,000 had been raised for the Holt agency. He'd be the first to admit that it wasn't just courage that allowed him to resist the obstacles and odds and finish his ride. He was convinced that his goal was one the Lord had given him. His cross-country trek was living out of his commitment to Jesus.

In spite of the inspiring examples of Dan Stocker and others, ours is a generation short on "spiritual heroes." The courageous qualities that drew the masses to the Messiah are missing from too many churches and individuals. But heroes can be grown. Though an endangered species, they are far from extinct.

Courage Up Close

Coming to terms with our own courageous instincts (or lack of them) is possible when we are sitting in the Lord's presence on a regular basis. I hope you are continuing to do that as you read God's Word and prayerfully journal each day of this 50-Day Spiritual Adventure. Praying with a pencil is a refreshingly different way to think of the routine of quiet time. It calls us to listen more than usual to what the Lord has to say. Jotting down thoughts that come to our head can betray fears and hopes that are hiding in our heart. Putting a pencil to paper as we visualize ourselves in the presence of God also increases the likelihood that we will continue to chew on some aspect of a Bible passage that the Holy Spirit causes to stand out.

As you establish a pattern of keeping a pencil and pad with you when you pray, you'll find yourself writing down goals and dreams you didn't know you had. You'll also be able to make lists of fears that hold you back from taking steps toward that God-breathed mission for your life.

You'll be able to record instances when the courage you see displayed in Jesus' life has cropped up in your own.

In fact, right now, put this book down and find a scrap of paper and something to write with. Take five minutes to write down five to ten accomplishments you have achieved that you would never have believed possible 10 years ago. As you withdraw those items from your memory bank, thank the Lord for giving you the desire and the courage to fulfill the goals he planted in your heart.

Two thousand years after the Cross, whenever the courage of Jesus is reflected in his people, others take notice. And sometimes that notice is rendered in unlikely places. Several years ago, Mel Gibson strayed from his typical role to play William Wallace, the great Scottish revolutionary in Randall Wallace's epic adventure film, *Braveheart*.

Even though Randall Wallace is a professed Christian and a distant relative of the film's hero (and a participant in Fuller Seminary's Reel Theology symposium), he did not shy away from graphic detail. Let me warn you, *Braveheart* is one of the bloodiest, most violent films I have ever seen. In a recent screening of a video clip in an adult Sunday school class, due to the graphic portrayal of a public execution, some adults looked down. Others had to leave the room. Still, in this remarkable motion picture, Randall Wallace wove unmistakable theological threads throughout the script. His portrayal of human redemption and political emancipation captures some of what Jesus spiritually accomplished on our behalf.

While the townspeople gather to witness his execution, Wallace is unmercifully tortured before being given an opportunity to deny his convictions and pledge allegiance to an unjust king. Because he refuses, the gut-wrenching torture routine is repeated. Once the king's legates are convinced of Wallace's determined defiance, they signal the hooded executioner. As the executioner raises a sharpened sword with which he will sever Wallace's head from his body, the victim cries, "Fre-e-e-e-dom!" And throughout the city, Wallace's prophetic voice continues its haunting echo. It is a chilling scene, but, unless you are very sensitive, I think it's well worth the wincing (and the price of video rental).

The scene on Golgotha was chilling as well. The dark clouds of impending tragedy cast an icy shadow over all of Jerusalem. Eyewitnesses reported that the sky went black as crimson blood pooled at the foot of the cross. In spite of the profound work of redemption that was staged, those who watched the original passion play were not aware of its significance. They were clueless about the spiritual freedom being purchased before their eyes. But perhaps they were amazed at the courage Jesus displayed as he succumbed to the cruelest form of death known to man—Roman crucifixion, involving open wounds, bleeding flesh, spiked hands and feet, moans, groans, and gasps from the one hung out to die while those who did the killing jeered and sneered.

Each torturous breath Jesus took required him to place all his weight on his spiked feet in order to slide his raw and bleeding back up the splintered wood of the vertical stake, all the while nailed to the horizontal beam. But though it was excruciating for him to catch a breath, the painful execution didn't catch Jesus by surprise. He knew in advance how his life would end.

That, you see, is another reason why Jesus was The People's Choice. Knowing what was in store, he stayed the course without attempting revenge or dodging the mission for which the Father had called him. And his awesome courage and focused purpose awed the masses.

I love the way the apostle Peter describes the restraint that accompanied Jesus' resolve to fulfill his sacred mission: "To this you were called because Christ suffered for you, leaving you an example. . . . When they hurled their insults at him, he did not retaliate; when he suffered, he made no threats. Instead, he entrusted himself to him who judges justly" (1 Peter 2:21–23).

> **Perhaps they were amazed at the courage Jesus displayed as he succumbed to the cruelest form of death known to man.**

The Christian adventure is not one that simply celebrates Jesus' accomplishments from a safe distance. While we do gather as his followers on a regular basis in places called "sanctuaries," our mission in life is not expressed within the security of stained-glass settings. It is lived out in the asphalt jungle of high-rise penthouses, low-rent districts, and middle-class suburbs, where fear stalks its prey and threatens to steal our lunch. The world in which we live out our faith comes complete with incomplete answers. It lacks airtight explanations or fairytale endings. At times, our task of shadowing the Savior is frightening— even painful. But if we are walking in the way of Jesus, we will find ourselves fulfilling a mission that is incredibly attractive to others.

There's a hymn we don't sing much anymore,

which has lyrics that articulate the hunger for courageously fulfilling a mission. It's the same hunger that marked the first-century disciples. It's obviously the desire that marked Jesus. And it should also mark those of us who run the race of faith in the twenty-first century.

> Teach me Your way, O Lord, teach me
>   Your way.
> Your guiding grace afford. Teach me Your
>   way.
> Help me to walk aright,
>   more by faith, less by sight.
> Lead me with heavenly light. Teach me
>   Your way. . . .
> Long as my life shall last, teach me Your
>   way.
> Where'er my lot be cast, teach me Your
>   way.
> Until the race is run,
>   until the journey's done,
> until the crown is won, teach me Your way.

> *(B. Mansell Ramsey, "Teach Me Your Way,"
> stanzas 1 and 4, © George Taylor, The Cross
> Printing Works, Stainland, Halifax, 1919.)*

For Discussion:

1. Is courage a quality you ordinarily think of in relationship to Jesus? Why or why not?

2. Describe a time in your life when you were forced to muster up every ounce of moral courage you had within you.

3. Do you think a person is more or less apt to be courageous when his or her life lacks clear direction? Why?

4. What is your mission in life? If you aren't sure, how can you begin to identify your life purpose?

5. What effect might perseverance and courage in fulfilling your mission have on those around you? How can this point them to Jesus?

Freedom

Lost.
Afraid.
Alone.
The dungeon's darkness
was my home.
Pitch-black blindness
robbed me of my vision.
Like a quilt of heavy steel,
the heavy weight of guilt
crushed my gasping soul.
But wait!
A shaft of light.
A keyhole-sized beam.
The prince of night
surrenders his keys
and with the turn of a lock
and the clank of an opening iron door,
golden sunlight floods the room.
At long last I am free.

—gea

CHAPTER EIGHT

Lights! Camera! Action!

ON A COLD NOVEMBER AFTERNOON in 1965, the Big
Apple was shaken to the core. Not by an earth-
quake—by a power outage. The blackout was felt in
Times Square and beyond. Over 80 thousand
square miles were affected. Somewhere in upstate
New York, a breakdown had occurred in a complex
power network that channels electricity to 30 million people from New York to Canada and from
Lake Huron to Boston. The much-heralded blackout of '65 didn't just last for a few minutes; it was
five and a half hours before power was restored.
For dozens of people trapped in an elevator 25
floors up the Empire State building, it probably felt
like five and a half days. And it was just as frightening for the estimated 600 thousand people stuck
in subways underground and underwater.

Journalist Loudon Wainwright described the
incident with artistic flair: "At 5:28 New York
winked as if someone had pulled the plug of a
Christmas tree. The great city of the sparkling
skyline and the glittering avenues went black—
suddenly revealing an alien beauty of stone and
steel looming dark against the sky. Then a full
moon rose to light a city beset by the most massive power failure in history."

Curiously, Wainwright discovered that New Yorkers handled the blackout of '65 amazingly well. He wrote that the people managed to carry on their business with splendid gaiety; in fact, the blackout seemed to transform the folks of New York. While in the light they had been strangers to one another, the darkness produced a kind of warmth and concern for other human beings in their difficult predicament. In that heart-touching five hours, wrote the journalist, "as they came down the great office buildings in little night processions led by men with flash-lights and candles, people held hands with those they could not see."

A blackout is one thing. The eternal night of spiritual alienation is another. Jesus entered a depraved world that was deprived of light. Darkness draped the bluish planet in a third-rate solar system to which Christ descended as the human embodiment of the invisible Creator. It was a world in which the poor were mistreated, prophets were stoned, children were sacrificed, truth was scoffed, pleasure was sought, and pros-titutes were bought. It was an unenlightened world where Caesars demanded worship and reli-gious leaders paraded their pride. The blind and the lame were shamed as scum. So, too, the lep-ers and mentally handicapped. And what was worse, those who disregarded the cadence of the culture in order to march to the drumbeat of their moral conscience were unable to get very far. Blinded by the darkness, they stumbled on, unable to penetrate the cosmic canopy that sepa-rated them from the God they longed to know.

The finite dimensions of a world infected by sin's virus offered little hope. Darkness reigned. Shrouded by clouds that camouflaged the

marionette strings of an evil puppeteer by the
name of Satan, humanity longed for freedom.

Letting in the Light

I will admit, I'm not a Jim Carey fan. I find his
humor offensive and his choice of movie scripts
questionable. But our family had heard so many
good things about *The Truman Show*, we decided
to rent the film when it finally came out on video.
If you haven't seen it, you owe it to yourself. It is
rich with spiritual symbolism. If you saw it and
wonder if I am in my right mind, watch it again
after considering this entry from my journal:

> *The Truman Show* is a strange movie that
> illustrates freedom from a life controlled by
> Satan. In the film a director by the name of
> Christof has created the world's largest
> sound stage in southern California simulat-
> ing an island community in the Pacific
> Ocean. For over 25 years a soap opera-type
> television show is broadcast 24 hours a day
> from this simulated community. The star
> of the show is Truman Burbank. From the
> time he was born, his entire life has been
> watched by millions of Americans on TV.
> But Truman doesn't know there is a camera
> capturing his every move. He doesn't know
> that his entire life is being choreographed
> by Christof. He is unaware that his choices
> are scripted and his perceived options are
> non-existent. Even the apparent sunshine
> overhead is a fake.
>
> In the darkness of his controlled exis-
> tence, Truman is blind to reality. Only as
> he begins to act on his hunches does he
> find the courage to test life as it appears

and eventually break from Christof. Once outside the artificial world of a Hollywood soundstage, Truman Burbank tastes the unimaginable flavor of freedom and feels the incomparable warmth of a real sun. Here is a film that celebrates the power of being set free from the puppet-like fate of those who are prisoners to the power of evil.

What *The Truman Show* portrays is the essence of our Easter faith. When Jesus defied the gravitational pull of the grave, he defeated death. When he pushed the stone away from the entrance to his borrowed tomb, the light from outside filled the empty cave. What a brilliant picture of spiritual darkness surrendering to the conquering light! In a way, the grave in which Jesus was sealed is a metaphor for the countless centuries before his birth that were defined by unenlightened chaos. God seemed distant. At times he was eerily silent. Disease and war, infanticide and slavery, promiscuity and power-driven, godless kings plagued the planet.

Jesus broke the power of darkness so all can live in the light.

No one could be sure if life beyond the grave was in the cards. But once the massive boulder was pried away from the mouth of that stone-cold death chamber, a world of possibilities that no one ever dreamed possible came into being. Then came that monumental weekend when the Creator recalibrated the cosmos. Really! Good Friday and Easter are more than holidays on the calendar. They are the bookends of our faith.

In *A Prayer for Owen Meany* (the book on which the popular film *Simon Birch* is based), John Irving wrote it so very well:

> I find that Holy Week is draining; no matter how many times I have lived through his crucifixion, my anxiety about his resurrection is undiminished—I am terrified that, this year, it won't happen; that, that year, it didn't. Anyone can be sentimental about the Nativity; any fool can feel like a Christian at Christmas. But Easter is the main event; if you don't believe in the resurrection, you're not a believer. (*The Jesus I Never Knew,* copyright © 1995 by Philip Yancey, Zondervan Publishing House, Grand Rapids, Mich., p. 207.)

As wonderful as Christmas is culturally, as significant as the Incarnation is theologically, the birth of Christ means nothing without the events that attend the end of his life. On the cross, Jesus staked his life on what he taught for the three years of his public ministry: that he is the Light of the World, that he is the Bread of Life, that he is the Living Water, that he is the Son of God, and that whoever believes in him will not perish but have eternal life. Because of the Cross, the Kingdom of God has burst into our broken world, and we can know forgiveness of sins and have an intimate relationship with the Father. It is on the cross that Jesus made good on all his parables and miracles.

But it is also on the cross that Jesus died. His claims were quenched by the blood that filled his lungs as he suffocated on the Roman stake to which he was torturously spiked. Death. Silence.

Weeping. Cheering. Better bury the body before the sun goes down.

In an upper room, the disciples nearly drowned in a pool of tears. Questions. Doubts. Regrets. Fears. They bolted the door, unsure of their own safety. While outside, Sabbath preparations continued routinely, with footsteps in the streets, laughter in the homes. Life went on even after the Life went off.

Who could say if what the rabbi from Nazareth said was the gospel truth? Certainly not his followers. They were clueless.

Sabbath preparations continued, with footsteps in the streets, laughter in the homes. Life went on even after the Life went off.

And then the clue was given. Picture it: The early morning mission to the cemetery is aborted. You can't sprinkle spices on a body in a grave if there is no body. The women flee with spices in hand, bewildered and afraid. All run except for Mary. And when the gardener calls her by name, she's ready to flee, too. But when it dawns on her who is speaking her name, her urge to run becomes an overwhelming desire to worship. Falling on her knees, she reaches out to embrace Jesus' feet. She is overcome with joy. She is overwhelmed with gratitude.

"Don't touch me!" a smiling Jesus cautions. "But do go and tell the others what you've seen. Tell the disciples—and Peter—that I am alive!"

See what I mean when I say Good Friday and Easter are the bookends of our faith? Redemption's story is bound to be understood only as we grasp what brackets it. The realities Jesus died claiming he proved true by reversing the curse of death. Easter validated Jesus' assertion on the cross that all that was necessary to accomplish an eternal relationship with our Creator was "finished."

The Greek word translated "It is finished" actually is a banking term. *Tetelestai* means "paid in full." Jesus redeemed us from spiritual bondage by paying a ransom the justice of a holy God demanded. Mission accomplished!

Overcoming Sin's Long Night

Not too long ago, I rewrote the words to "Twinkle, Twinkle, Little Star" so that kids in our church might be able to understand on their level what Jesus has accomplished by coming into our world as the light of the world. Here's how it goes:

> Twinkle, twinkle, Morning Star.
> Holy Jesus, God you are.
> To our world you came as light,
>   overcoming sin's long night.
> Twinkle, twinkle, Morning Star.
> Holy Jesus, God you are.

That concept of overcoming sin's long night is a deep one for adults, let alone preschoolers, to consider. But as I've suggested before, metaphor and storytelling can help.

My kids have an animated version of C. S. Lewis's *The Lion, the Witch, and the Wardrobe* on video. I'm captivated by the scene in which Aslan the lion (a Christ-figure) is tied to the stone table and a dagger is thrust through his heart. The evil queen screams with delight. The rightful heir to the kingdom of Narnia will no longer pose a threat to her reign of icy darkness.

But wait—a deafening sound is heard. A loud

crack is traced to the stone table. Strangely, the corpse of the lion is gone. All that remains is the table of execution broken into two equal parts. The queen stops her victory dance. Has her celebration been premature?

Then the colorless, frozen wasteland of what she thought was an invincible kingdom begins to thaw. The gray hues of a somber world dominated by darkness surrender to the polychromatic splendor of living color. When the stone table cracked, Aslan broke the queen's dreaded spell. No longer dead, his presence proves his redemptive death reversed the curse under which Narnia had languished. Narnia is Eden once again.

Obviously, we still live in a world that bears little resemblance to the garden-like paradise God created. Because Jesus broke the power of darkness, our globe has been wired with the capability of spiritual illumination. But that doesn't mean all the light bulbs are in place or all the light switches have been flipped to the "on" position. We are surrounded by the consequences of sin. I like the way my poet friend Bryan Jeffery Leech puts it. "We have lived in the shade of the dark we have made, when He wills us to walk in the light." And we continue to live in the shadows, even after the darkness of our own making has been forgiven.

I enjoy watching movies in the afternoon. For one thing, now that I'm pushing fifty, there is a much better chance I'll stay awake through the whole film or video if I see it before 6:00 at night. (Watching a movie after a big evening meal in a restaurant has given me a degree of empathy for those who struggle to stay awake through my sermons. It can be agonizing!)

Anyway, if you've been to a matinee movie,

you know that when you leave the darkened theater, it takes a while for your eyes to adjust to the
brightness of the outdoors. That's a crude way of
explaining why we have difficulty seeing the consequences of Jesus' defeat of darkness. We live in a
time of adjustment. Our spiritual eyes are adjust-
ing to a kingdom that has come but isn't fully
here. We are living in the period when what is
perceived is being calibrated with what we believe.

**We are living in the period when
what is perceived is being calibrated with what we believe.**

The power of darkness has been broken, but
we are still broken people living in a broken
world where sinful people willfully make sinful
choices. And what makes our world seem even
darker is that too many Christians are blind to
the enlightening presence of God the resurrection
of Jesus makes possible. They've closed their eyes
to his mercies that dawn new every morning. The
obstacles of doubt and disbelief limit our exposure to the available light of God's presence. The
craters of guilt and regret loom larger than we
think, creating those shadows Bryan wrote about.

But through Jesus, we have light to see the
face of God and recognize the smile that vali-
dates our identity as his children. We can see in
order to carry on under the circumstances of a
kingdom that has not yet fully come.

When I was a sophomore at Seattle Pacific
University, a power outage hit our sister school,
Westmont College in Santa Barbara. The campus
was crippled by the absence of light. You see,
Westmont is a hilly place, with dorms and class-
room buildings dotted among the cypress and

eucalyptus trees. Without streetlights illuminating the narrow paths that connect the campus, you might as well forget trying to find your way.

Several weeks after the outage, we had a guest from Westmont visit our school. Ray told about the frightening experience they had lived through. But a smile crossed his face as he spoke of a blind student named Charlene who found herself an unsuspecting hero. Charlene was known and loved by the student body. She was so comfortable with her handicap, her peers forgot she couldn't see.

More than once, other students would enter her room and be taken by surprise to find Charlene sitting at her desk in the pitch dark, typing away on a term paper. Because she was sightless, a power outage did not impair Charlene's ability to get around campus. Unlike her seeing friends, she was not dependent upon electricity to light the walks and trails. While hundreds of students lit candles and huddled together in their dorms, Charlene went on with her life as usual and tried to help others do the same. Fortunately, she had a manual typewriter.

> He sets us free to explore the future as if it is a spiritual adventure, because it is. Our entire lives are a spiritual adventure.

When Ray told us about Charlene, I had an insight about what it's like being a Christian in a world that is not yet the paradise Jesus promised. Most of those who inhabit our planet are paralyzed by spiritual darkness, even though Jesus has made the necessary connections so they can live illuminated lives. But for those of us who have claimed the gift of eternal life, we have an ability to get along that others do not have.

What makes Jesus so attractive? He has broken the power of darkness so we can live in the light. Another quality that attracts us to the living Christ is the way he responds to us when we refuse to live in his light. He patiently considers all the logical reasons we throw at him for why we are whistling in the dark as we are, and what does he do? He counters all our excuses and exposes our ignorance. But in the process, he proves that we don't have to live dim lives. He sets us free to explore the future as if it is a spiritual adventure, because it is. Our entire lives—not just a certain 50 days—are a spiritual adventure.

John Wesley is one of the most famous Christians in history. He lived about the same time as George Washington. While Washington was leading Colonial troops against the British in America, Wesley was fighting the forces of evil in England. He was a traveling evangelist who founded the Methodist church. Wesley's journal bears witness to his own spiritual adventure. He writes of his heart being strangely warmed upon his conversion.

Thanks to Wesley, we have a tried-and-true method for grounding new Christians in the faith: small groups. Maybe you have taken advantage of small groups during the 50-Day Adventure and can witness to the growth that has resulted in your life. Let me encourage you to stay plugged into a cadre of caring Christians with whom you can be open and pray and to whom you can be held accountable in areas of your life that need tough love.

John Wesley's brother Charles was also a preacher, but we are more familiar with him as a poet. His poetry has been put to music and sung by Christians around the world. Charles Wesley wrote over 2,000 hymns. Thanks to John Wesley's brother, we have a vocabulary with which to describe the freedom Jesus Christ provided us through his defeat of death. Listen to these familiar words from a great old hymn of the church called "And Can It Be?" See if they don't characterize what Jesus did for you when he broke the power of darkness and freed you from the prison of self, allowing you to step into the light of God's love:

> *Long my imprisoned spirit lay*
> *Fast bound in sin and nature's night.*
> *Thine eye diffused a quickening ray;*
> *I woke—the dungeon flamed with light!*
> *My chains fell off, my heart was free,*
> *I rose, went forth and followed Thee.*

I'm taken by that phrase *the dungeon flamed with light*. What a powerful image! A cell defined as a windowless hell is defined that way no longer. There's freedom. There's fresh air and sunlight. There's life!

This week, as I've contemplated the dungeon of death into which the cold, stiff, lifeless body of Jesus was placed, I've imagined that dungeon flamed with light. Whether or not Jesus departed before the stone was rolled away from the tomb is immaterial. Most likely, the stone was rolled away to let the disciples in, not to let Jesus out. But picture the scene on the canvas of your mind. Once the boulder that blocked the entrance to the tomb was gone, so was the darkness. The stench of death escaped. The bright rays of the morning sun streamed into the cave, giving a golden hue to the limestone walls. The earthworms, beetles, and potato bugs scurried for cover. The long, dark night of the Savior's soul was over.

The earthworms, beetles, and potato bugs scurried for cover. The long, dark night of the Savior's soul was over.

The power of the Resurrection hit home several years ago on an Easter Sunday morning. It began with an outdoor sunrise service. The well-bundled crowd gathered at the corner of our church property, where a tall cross reached toward the pre-dawn sky. After someone read the passages relating to the events of Good Friday, the crowd proceeded across the church parking lot toward a footbridge, singing, "Were you there when they laid him in the tomb?" The procession was led by two men carrying what appeared to be a linen-wrapped corpse on a stretcher. In actuality, it was a volleyball and a couple of bulk mail containers tightly wrapped in old bed sheets.

Once we reached the footbridge, those who carried the "body" deposited it near a creek in a culvert that looked like a first-century tomb. The effect was fantastic! We then continued our sunrise march serpentine beyond the bridge to a grove of olive trees. The service ended with a young woman dressed in first-century garb running from the culvert, calling, "He is risen!" We sang "Our God Reigns" and shared the Easter confession of the earliest believers: "Christ is risen! He is risen indeed!"

As we dismissed, the sun emerged over the nearby hillside. It was an unforgettable experience.

Because I still had to go home and dress for

two traditional services in the sanctuary, I decided to retrieve "the body" after the morning's final service. But, come noon, I was so tired and hungry, I took off for a restaurant to meet my family for Easter brunch. While eating my Denver omelet, it dawned on me that I had forgotten the corpse at the creek.

By the time I returned to the church after brunch, "the body" was gone! I looked everywhere. There was no trace of it anywhere. Could someone on the road have seen the suspicious shape in the creek and called the police? My imagination would not quit. However, my exhaustive search did end—unsuccessfully. As I drove home, I had to laugh. God had allowed me to experience something of what the original cast of Easter felt when they found a body missing.

Continuing Jesus' Ministry

A missing volleyball is one thing. In the case of Jesus, the body wasn't missing; it was living! The world that woke one Sunday morning in the darkness of spiritual night did not go to bed in the same predicament. The power of darkness had been broken once and for all.

Just ask the apostle Paul. Tutored by Gamaliel, a greatly respected first-century teacher, Paul grew up blinded by an arrogant sense of his own importance. He had learned much from his knowledgeable mentor, but the darkness of spiritual ignorance and willful pride earned him an *F* in Salvation 101. He probably never heard Jesus preach. He presumably never saw the charismatic Carpenter performed a miracle. But he was only too aware of those who had.

The contagion of Christians in Jerusalem was resulting in many converts. It was giving the established religious leaders migraine headaches, Paul included. Instead of taking pain killers, Paul took murderous action. From what we can surmise from Scripture, Paul went on the offensive to wipe out as many Christians as he could.

Talk about living in the darkness! Standing in the shadows, Paul consented to the public execution of Stephen. It could be that he supervised those who stoned the young deacon. Christians fled town. Not easily distracted, Paul headed toward Damascus on horseback to round up as many disciples of Jesus as he could find. His intent was to brand them as heretics and return them to a Jerusalem jail until they suffered the same fate as Stephen.

But the risen Jesus had his own intentions. As with Peter and Matthew and the others, Jesus saw Paul's potential, not his present status. He was determined to bring out the best in Paul. And so, with a shaft of light beamed from heaven, Jesus focused his love on Paul. The unlikely disciple was knocked off his high horse and blinded. A few days later, a devout believer living in Damascus laid his hands on Paul and prayed over him. As tears crawled down Paul's cheeks, scales fell from his eyes. The spiritual darkness those scales symbolized dissolved into the brilliance of a new birth.

Years later, Paul reflected on his conversion as he stood before King Agrippa in Caesarea. The words of Jesus he'd heard on the Damascus road 20 years before still rang with clarity in Paul's ears:

> "I have appeared to you to appoint you as
> a servant and as a witness of what you
> have seen of me and what I will show you.
> I will rescue you from your own people
> and from the Gentiles. I am sending you

to them to open their eyes and turn them from darkness to light, and from the power of Satan to God, so that they may receive forgiveness of sins and a place among those who are sanctified by me." (Acts 26:16–18)

Paul's mission as a Christian was nothing less than a continuation of Jesus' ministry. Paul knew his purpose was helping people find the light switch so their worlds could be illuminated, just like his had been.

Paul's mission as a Christian was nothing less than a continuation of Jesus' ministry. And our purpose should be the same.

And our purpose should be the same. Our lives are not being broadcast from coast to coast as a camera trains its lens on our every move. But we are like Truman Burbank. More people are watching our lives than we can imagine: The mail carrier. The pharmacist. The kid who delivers the newspaper. The convenience store clerk. The pro at the golf course. And don't forget the neighbors. If they know we claim to be Christians, you can bet they are looking for ways our professed faith in Jesus affects our attitudes, responses, and behavior. If they see an *ichthus* decal on the rear bumper of our car, they may try to bait us, just to gauge our reaction to life's little—and big—challenges.

Yes, we are like Truman Burbank. But we can also be like Westmont's Charlene by taking the lead and inviting others to follow. How are you doing with Action Step 2? Have you dedicated your home as a lighthouse of prayer? It's a simple yet tangible way to continue Christ's mission, purposefully living out your faith before others in your sphere of influence.

Praying for those on your block or on your floor will help you look differently at those who stumble through life in spiritual darkness. It is more difficult to be unloving toward people you talk to God about. Asking other churchgoers in your neighborhood to join you to pray for concerns in your community or at the local public schools could intensify the brightness of your lighthouse's beam. Don't be bothered that they don't go to your church or belong to your particular denomination. When it comes to God answering prayer, doctrinal compatibility is not a prerequisite.

Lighthouses of prayer are a natural consequence of our belief that the risen Christ desires to live out his life-changing power through his followers. Our faith hinges on the darkness-shattering reality of Easter Sunday. No wonder we keep coming back to a pitch-black cave that has been pierced by the light. When we rehearse the script of the Resurrection, we are reminded why people of hope continuously celebrate Jesus. In the empty tomb, we find the bottom-line validation of our faith. It is a gift as primal as the discovery of fire by descendants of Adam who dwelled in dark, stone caves.

Sadly, though, not everyone accepts the gift. Those unconvinced that the Easter chapter in the Christian story is true would question the premise of this book. They're not at all sure Jesus really is the popular hero history has painted him to be. Sure, he had his followers and much applause, but he had more than his share of sorrows, too.

His life, they claim, was a tragedy of tragedies—one for the books. They quote chapter and verse, where Jesus spoke of the need to eat his body and drink his blood and the repulsed crowd rejected his teaching and stopped hanging around him. They seize on Jesus' non-member status of the orthodox religious establishment. They underscore his betrayal at the hand of one of his trusted Twelve and his rejection by the crowd, which cried out for his execution and the release of the renowned criminal Barabbas. They remind us that another of his faithful followers cursed and spit and denied even knowing the convicted King of the Jews.

> Those who tally the score at the ninth hour on Good Friday forget it was only the top of the ninth inning.

Jesus' critics are quick to point out that he died alone, mocked and maligned, on a barren hill on a stormy day. They see the end of his life as the defining moment. Sure, many had applauded Jesus. But, in the end, his biography was shelved under the category of many sorrows and unkept promises. The censors view his life as just another underexposed snapshot in the historical album of people walking in darkness, longing for the light.

But those who tally the score at the ninth hour on Good Friday forget it was only the top of the ninth inning. Preoccupied with apparent failure and loss, they forget that's the way the ball bounces on an imperfect, sin-infested planet. Sure, there are a lot of bad plays. But don't give up on the home team! The bottom of the ninth had yet to be played. There was an extended rain delay and then . . . look out! Earthquakes, angels, rolling stones, and death-defying feats. If you wait long enough, the applause drowns out the sorrows.

If you have ever watched a Billy Graham Crusade on TV, you've heard Cliff Barrows, at the end of the broadcast, make mention of how easy it is to send correspondence to Dr. Graham. Billy Graham, Minneapolis, Minnesota. That's all the address you need.

In the Billy Graham Museum on the campus of Wheaton College is an exhibit of humorously addressed letters that have been sent to the world's most celebrated evangelist. One letter in particular stands out from the rest. Sent from a viewer in Nigeria, in the place of the simple address, it reads, "Billy Graham, Many Applause, Many Sorrows."

On one level, this phonetic rendering of a familiar address unfamiliar to an African listener is quite funny. (It reminds me of how a boy in my daughter's second-grade class pronounced our last name: "Apples on my cocoa list.") But on another level, such an address is ironically appropriate. Billy Graham is not the only one who resides at that residence. In a fallen world, Many Applause, Many Sorrows is where we all live.

That is the way of the world this side of heaven. Even for Jesus. But because of the Resurrection, the applause that attended Jesus at his birth, throughout his public ministry, and at the beginning of Holy Week is not dwarfed by the many sorrows that snuffed out his life. We have every reason to believe that when he strode out of the grave, the hosts of heaven gave him a standing ovation. It is an ovation that continues, joined by all who have entered in his presence, a standing ovation that will attend his reign in the Eternal City to come. There, "every knee shall bow and every tongue confess that Jesus Christ is Lord to the glory of God the Father" (Philippians 2:10–11). Talk about The People's Choice!

The People's Choice has given his people a challenge. Those of us called out of darkness into his marvelous light are entrusted with a sacred mission to remove whatever obstacles prevent others from basking in the brilliance of God's unconditional acceptance.

Before the days of electricity, streets were illuminated by gas lamps attached to tall poles strategically positioned every so many feet. When Robert Louis Stevenson was a boy, his favorite pastime early each evening was to lean on the windowsill of his second story bedroom and watch the lamplighter make his daily appearance.

The lamplighter would raise his long torch to light the wick of each lamp, one after another. Not quite able to understand how it all worked, Stevenson is reported to have said to his parents, "Look, outside. It's the man who punches holes in the darkness!"

More than 600 years before the first Easter, Isaiah wrote, "The people walking in darkness have seen a great light; on those living in the land of the shadow of death a light has dawned" (Isaiah 9:2). Because of Jesus' defeat of death, the light that came into our world when the Word became flesh continues to shine (John 1:1–14).

An eternal flame was lit that first Easter. But, unlike the eternal flame that burns continually at the grave of former President Kennedy in Arlington National Cemetery, the flame of which I write does not burn at some highly trafficked tourist stop. More powerful than a literal torch, the flame I have in mind is the spiritual fire that is blazing a trail into the future of our world. It's a flame that burns confidence into our hearts. Its flicker will one day spread like a forest fire, purging the world of injustice, hate, and unrequited wrong, illuminating every shadowed valley and every life dimmed by sin's darkness.

And we are the keepers of the flame. Using the metaphor of young Robert Louis Stevenson, we have been given the incredible privilege of finding ways to punch holes in the darkness of our apathetic, unbelieving world and let the light—the Light—shine through.

For Discussion:

1. What attitude do you think people in your sphere of influence have toward the Resurrection?

2. Do you find the idea of light conquering darkness effective? Why or why not?

3. Besides an event that brought light into darkness, what analogy would you use to describe what Jesus did when he rose from the dead?

4. Have you ever brought light into a situation or to the life of someone you know? What happened?

5. Into what circumstances in your life might you be able to bring the light of Christ in the months ahead? How?

Every Knee Shall Bow

In the name of campaigning,
integrity bows to image.
Polls dictate policy.
Money buys votes.
Even the visages
of the candidates
rate higher than their views.
The people's choices
will always win
but the way they win,
we lose.
At the name of Jesus,
everyone will one day
bow down—
those who praise him
as Savior and Lord
and those who
(fearing judgment)
will frown.
And because that day
soon approaches,
our adventure exceeds 50 days.
To lobby His cause,
to convince the unsure,
so in bowing
they'll offer Him praise.

—gea

Epilogue

IN HIS BOOK *The Jesus I Never Knew,* Phil Yancey makes reference to a forged document purported to be written by Publius Lentulus, the Roman governor who succeed Pontius Pilate. The document, actually written in 1514, includes a physical description of Jesus Christ:

> He is a tall man, well shaped and of an amiable and reverend aspect; his hair is of a color that can hardly be matched, falling into graceful curls . . . parted on the crown of his head, running as a stream to the front after the fashion of the Nazarites; his forehead high, large and imposing; his cheeks without spot or wrinkle, beautiful with a lovely red; his nose and mouth formed with exquisite symmetry; his beard, and of a color suitable to his hair, reaching below his chin and parted in the middle like a fork; his eyes bright blue, clear and serene. (*The Jesus I Never Knew,* copyright © 1995 by Philip Yancey, Zondervan Publishing House, Grand Rapids, Mich., p. 86.)

When I read that, I said to myself, "Sure sounds like a candidate running for political office." You know what I mean? Every hair in place. Great complexion. Attractive. After all, it seems candidates have to be capable of passing a screen test in order to make it past the primaries. At least they have to know how much makeup base to put on before making a televised appearance. Image is everything.

Every election year, candidates blitz the country with the goal of becoming the people's choice. Millions of dollars are spent creating a sellable candidate. (And *sellable* isn't just a figure of speech.) Campaigners write speeches for public appeal and design media ads with sex appeal. Direct mail specialists engineer solicitations to leave the voters with just the right impression.

Sadly, the candidates often prove unfaithful to the policies they have publicly pledged allegiance to in the company of many witnesses. A beguiling bedfellow proves irresistible; the name of the temptress is Image.

But the public at large is just as guilty. We get carried away with the hype and image and fail to inform ourselves of the facts. Impressed with looks or style or the graphics on billboards, we vote our preferences instead of our convictions. And then, once the election is over and the enthusiasm fades, our support flags, and the banners we carried disappear.

In the case of supporting Jesus, image is not all that important. Isaiah's prophetic view of the Messiah reflected One who was somewhat homely and physically unattractive. (Quite unlike the description from the sixteenth-century document.) Beside his appearance, Jesus' substance was unfiltered. His views were not always popular. Unlike politicians of our day, Jesus expressed his opinion before hiring a pollster to find out what the people wanted him to say. But in the end, that honest, straightforward conviction and courage is what won him history's homage.

Celebrating Jesus has nothing to do with the hype of a pre-election campaign rally. It is more than emotional momentum that may be the result of a seven-week, eight-Sunday, all-church event that I hope has produced accelerated spiritual growth in your life. Celebrating Jesus is a way of life that is not restricted to 50 days. So, now that the 50-Day Spiritual Adventure is coming to a close, the level of your allegiance to The People's Choice is about to be tested. Celebrating Jesus means voting for him every day of your life.

We vote with our feet—where we go and what we do. We vote with our arms—who we reach out to. We vote with our eyes—what we allow ourselves to be visually exposed to. We vote with our ears—what we listen to. We vote with our mouth—what we choose to say or not say. We vote with our calendar—what we prioritize and make room for in our busy lives. We vote with our wallet—what we value enough to spend our hard-earned cash on. Each day, we make decisions that determine how supportive we are of Jesus.

I received an e-mail from a member of a church I pastored years ago. She reflected on the apathy of so many within the church. A congregation that once was vibrant now struggles to maintain the status quo. Sundays are predictable. Participation is minimal. Jamie wrote,

> To me, it seems like a few take ownership of the church and the rest just show to take what is given. I thought a lot about that verse in the third chapter of Revelation, where Jesus wishes we were hot or cold instead of lukewarm. I've wondered, if Jesus were running for public office, where would we fit in? Would

we be on the platform supporting him, down in the crowd watching the show, having neighborhood teas to introduce him, promising to vote and then forgetting, or perhaps ignoring the election altogether? I'm convinced if we all went to church with the idea of giving ourselves and our resources to God and each other, the church would blossom far beyond anything we could imagine.

My friend Jamie is absolutely right. Perhaps if we viewed Jesus as an incumbent candidate running for reelection, personally seeking our support, we'd approach our daily routines and priorities a bit differently. If we believed that the level of our commitment to his campaign would influence countless others who are still undecided, we'd be more vocal and consistent in identifying who were are voting for.

Ultimately, it all comes down to this. There are many qualities that make Jesus the most attractive person ever. He is, without question, The People's Choice. But, whether he is The People's Choice or *your* choice depends on you. In the days to come, in order to mark your ballot decisively and vote purposefully, read up on the issues. Know where Jesus stands on them. Embrace the values he holds forth.

The end result will be a faith you will not be able to keep to yourself. Others will know for whom you're voting. The unconvinced will seek you out. And, come the day the results are tabulated, more will bow before the throne with worship on their lips, choosing him for themselves, than we ever thought possible.